the
st o r y
of
the
voice™

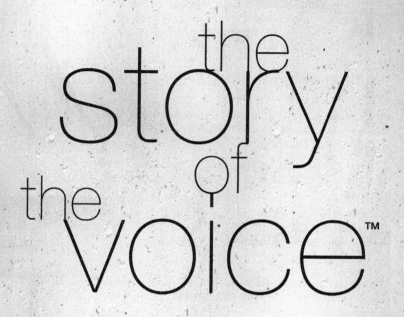

the story of the voice™

DAVID B. CAPES

WITH

CHRIS SEAY

AND

JAMES F. COUCH JR.

THOMAS NELSON
Since 1798

NASHVILLE DALLAS MEXICO CITY RÍO DE JANEIRO

Published in Nashville, Tennessee, by Thomas Nelson. Thomas Nelson is a registered trademark of Thomas Nelson, Inc.

Thomas Nelson, Inc., titles may be purchased in bulk for educational, business, fund-raising, or sales promotional use. For information, please e-mail SpecialMarkets@ThomasNelson.com.

ISBN: 978-1-4016-7668-1

Printed in the United States of America

13 14 15 16 17 RRD 5 4 3 2 1

table of contents

the story of the voice

acknowledgments

I want to thank Chris Seay for inviting me to come along for this long, slow journey through Scripture. It has been my privilege to serve as lead scholar on the project for Ecclesia Bible Society. Chris's vision for this project as well as his leadership have made this a great journey of discovery. Kelly Hall, whom we affectionately called Kelly Black Arrow, has become a good friend and colleague to many of us through these years. Her skills as both a poet and administrator have benefited this project in ways too many to count.

I am also grateful to Frank Couch and Maleah Bell of Thomas Nelson, who welcomed me to serve as a writer and reviewer for a good deal of the manuscript from the publisher's side. They were patient in teaching me, the professor, important aspects of the publishing business. The leadership at Thomas Nelson—Sam Moore, Michael Hyatt, Mark Schoenwald, and Gary Davidson—have demonstrated great vision and courage throughout the seven years it took to translate and develop The Voice and its other products. Their daring was even more pronounced given the strained economic conditions being experienced in the United States and around the world.

Since 2010 it has been my privilege to serve as the Thomas Nelson Research Professor at Houston Baptist University. This unique collaboration between the university and Thomas Nelson has enabled me to work with and for two great institutions simultaneously, hopefully for their mutual benefit. The concept came initially from Frank Couch in the summer of 2010. When he approached Dr. Robert Sloan, the president of HBU, with the proposal, Dr. Sloan was quick to see the advantages to HBU, Thomas Nelson, and me. I am grateful to Dr. Sloan for his good leadership.

I wish to thank my friend and colleague Dr. Larry Hurtado, retired professor of New Testament and former head of the School of Divinity at the University of Edinburgh. During fall 2009 I spent several months as a visiting fellow at the University of Edinburgh working through some of the longer prophetic and wisdom books. Those months in my basement flat one mile north of New College, in the School of Divinity library, and in the office they provided gave me a time of focused attention I could not have achieved elsewhere. Without this sabbatical granted by the trustees of HBU, I could never have met the manuscript deadlines. Additionally, the conversations with Larry and other colleagues at New College clarified for me a number of translation issues and made the final project stronger. The University of Edinburgh is truly a world-class university.

Finally, I want to thank my wife, Cathy, and my children, Bryan, Daniel, and Jordan. They have been supportive, encouraging, and understanding as this project took more of me away from them longer than anyone had anticipated. I'm grateful for their love and help during these years.

David B. Capes, *Thomas Nelson Research Professor*
Department of Theology
Houston Baptist University

In 2004 my pastor, Chris Seay, invited me to lunch at Saltgrass Steak-
house in Houston. It is a Texas-themed restaurant with horseshoes,
porcelain signs, farm implements, and other rusty reminders of kinder,
gentler times strategically hung on the walls. Over a good meal we had
pleasant conversation on a variety of topics. I did not really know what
was on his mind. Toward the end of the meal, he told me.

Chris had been thinking for years about the difficulties he faced
as a pastor in teaching the Scriptures using the available translations.
At times he found it helpful to write out the stories himself in a kind
of screenplay format, employing his own versions in sermons. He
was currently using Eugene Peterson's *The Message* to guide him, but
there were aspects of the translation that didn't resonate with him or
his audience. He told me he had been in conversations with a number
of people about the possibility of working on a new Bible translation.
He asked if I might have any interest in such a project. Because of my
own calling, and my admiration for Chris and his ministry, I was very
interested and asked him to tell me more.

First, Chris said, he wanted to establish Ecclesia Bible Society,
whose first priority would be to create a new Bible translation that
brought together scholars, writers, poets, and artists. Like me he
was concerned that some of the beauty, grit, and humor of the
Scriptures—and more significantly, the essential story of the Bible—
was obscured in other translations. The more I thought about the
approach, the more I saw how different this could be from other
translations and how valuable a resource it could be for the church.

The second thing Chris said was the clincher. After we talked
about the general idea and how it might work, we discussed one

potential outcome. If the project was successful, then Ecclesia Bible Society would use the royalties to "do good" in the world and extend the reach of God's kingdom. Already our church was involved in Latin America, Africa, and other places where extreme poverty and deprivation grips the populaces and where the gospel is heard only in muffled tones. We talked that day and since about how The Voice could be used to fund various mission projects such as drilling water wells in drought-stricken areas, fighting hunger and poverty, addressing the growing problem of human trafficking, and translating the Scriptures into other languages. Chris assured me that no one person or group of people would be the primary beneficiary of this effort. The true beneficiaries would be the poorest of the poor.

As we left the restaurant that day, I was ready. Had there been a dotted line, I would have signed. The notion that we might put the Scriptures into the hands of millions of people who would likely never pick up another translation intrigued and enticed me. Add to that idea the possibility that funds could be generated to do great good in the name of Jesus, and I was hooked.

This book attempts to tell part of the story of how The Voice Bible came to be. There will be gaps in the story, of course, because no one has access to all the people, all the details, all the correspondence, or all the minds of those who contributed one way or another to the project. In the end, anyone who reads this book will have a better sense of how The Voice Bible came to be and why.

One of my tasks since the release of The Voice in 2012 has been to manage a blog at the project's website, www.hearthevoice.com. I have written a majority of the posts, but from time to time I have asked some of our writers, friends, and scholars to write as well. I am grateful to each of those friends and colleagues who contributed in some way to this ongoing effort to tell the story. Throughout the book you will find excerpts from these blogs written by me and others embedded within the chapters. Since these posts were written in the moment and often in response to questions from critics, bloggers, and fans, they provide useful snapshots of how this project unfolded.

chapter

1

In the Beginning

Chris Seay is a third-generation pastor. Like most preachers' kids, he grew up seeing both the beauty and hypocrisy of the church. But unlike many, he chose to invest his life in the church and accomplish his Father's business rather than abandoning the church altogether. Whenever Chris and his family were faced with some bit of church messiness, Chris would seek his earthly father's counsel. The Reverend Ed Seay, after listening to his son's concerns, would tell Chris to go aside for a while and read the book of Acts. Ed knew that if his son could ever capture a vision of what the church is supposed to be, he would be able to work through the disappointments and make something beautiful happen.

In following God's call in his life, Chris attended Baylor University and began studying the Bible's original languages: Hebrew and Greek. He was especially inspired by one of his professors, Dr. Alan Culpepper. Culpepper is an expert in the literary style of the Fourth Gospel, the book of John. In conversations and classroom lectures, Chris began to discover the literary quality behind the Scriptures. But when Chris turned to the available Bible translations, he realized the beauty, poetry, and diversity of the Bible were not coming through. Modernity, it seems, values homogeneity. The modern approach takes the Bible as a single book rather than as a collection of sixty-six different books. In fact, the more Chris studied, the more he realized how important it is to understand that the Scripture is a library of sacred

1

material. It was then that he started longing for someone to offer a translation that would bring out the beauty, grit, and even humor of the Bible.

In the 1800s biblical studies became more specialized and technical. With the rise of the various "criticisms"—such as textual, historical, and source—biblical studies became the property of the academy rather than the church. The result was that English Bible translations published in the nineteenth and twentieth centuries were less literary and more technical works. Bible translation had become more about science than about art. As a result, the essential story of the Bible was lost.

Here was the problem with the modern translations.

The Vision for *The Voice*

When Chris was a student at Baylor, he started University Baptist Church in Waco, Texas with his close friend David Crowder. This unique church reached thousands of young people, utilizing passion for the arts, an authentic atmosphere, and a contagious passion for the story of Jesus. A few years later he and his wife, Lisa, moved to Houston and founded Ecclesia Houston. As Chris attempted to open the Scriptures each week in these churches, he discovered that modern translations tended to obscure the story; so he started writing out key parts of the Scripture as screenplays and having people read his own versions in worship. The response was immediately positive.

As modernity is giving way to a postmodern mind-set, it is important to understand that postmoderns—the kinds of people showing up weekly to worship at Ecclesia Houston and the thousands of churches like it—view the world differently; they process ideas differently. Rather than seeing Scripture as a list of propositions, postmoderns are returning the concept of story to the forefront of engaging Scripture. People connect with stories more than they do with isolated facts. Jesus taught through stories, parables, and metaphors; but some modern Christians have reduced his teaching to a system of irrefutable facts.

blog entry

September 26, 2011

The Power of the Story Reaches Us

by David Capes

We received a question on our Voice Facebook page from one of our fans.

> Question: "What is propositional-based thought and how does it apply to us?"

The fan is referring to the introduction in one of The Voice products where we observe that people do not respond to propositions as well as they respond to stories. This, of course, is nothing new. People have been telling stories for thousands of years. Humans are hard-wired to tell stories, remember them and pass them along to others.

Not long ago when people were sharing "the gospel," they would boil it down to a set of manageable propositions:

1. God loves you and has a wonderful plan for your life.
2. But you are a sinner separated from God.
3. Christ died for your sins and helps to bridge the gap between you and God.
4. So put your trust in Jesus to be saved.

Now these propositions are true, but they make little sense when isolated from the greater story of God's plan and purpose for the world and us.

3   *In the Beginning*

Let me illustrate it this way. Here are some lines from one of the greatest films of all time (*Casablanca* 1942):

> "Here's looking at you, kid."
> "Major Strasser has been shot. Round up the usual suspects."
> "Play it, Sam. Play 'As Time Goes By.'"
> "Of all the gin joints in all the towns in all the world and she walks into mine."
> "If that plane leaves the ground and you're not on it, you'll regret it. Maybe not today. Maybe not tomorrow. But soon and for the rest of your life."

Now these are some of the most memorable lines in the film. But without the rest of the story you have no clue what is going on. They might punctuate the story, remind you of the story, illustrate the story, but they are no substitute for the story itself.

Let's consider the question another way.

Imagine deciding whether or not to marry someone based on a resume. You might say, "Well, he looks good on paper." No. We would never do that. On a first date you don't exchange resumes or give a list of your strengths and weaknesses (you don't, that is, if you expect a second date!) No. You sit down over a good meal and begin to tell your story. You talk about where you come from, what you love to do, what it was like to be the older brother or sister in a family of four (or whatever is unique to your own story). This is how we woo a potential partner and how we make friends, by telling our unique stories to those willing to listen.

God did not give us a list of propositions to follow. He could have, but He didn't. Instead He gave us 66 books that detail an amazing story of love and redemption. Ecclesia Bible Society and Thomas Nelson have created The Voice Bible because they recognize the power of stories to tell the truth and call us into a new life.[1]

As Western culture moved into this period often described as *postmodernism*, Chris struggled to tell the whole story of God through the available translations. Formal translations may have gotten all the words right, but they missed the story. More contemporary translations and paraphrases seemed to have gotten the story right, but they were so trendy that ten years after they were published they sounded outdated.

When Ecclesia Houston gathered in the early 2000s, Chris generally used Eugene Peterson's translation, The Message, in his sermons. He found Peterson's version helpful, and the people to whom he was ministering week after week could identify with it . . . for the most part. In fact, it is not a stretch to suggest that The Message set a new direction in Bible translation and paved the way for Chris to imagine a new translation like The Voice that drew deeply from the Christian tradition and retold the story well to a contemporary audience. Indeed, as The Voice project began, Chris often cited something he had heard from Peterson, namely, that going forward each new generation has the responsibility of retelling the story of Scripture for a new audience.

When Chris shared his dissatisfaction with other pastors and church leaders, he found they shared many of the same frustrations and challenges. He often said that he wished someone would do something about the problem. Eventually one of his friends said, "I think you are that 'someone.'" Chris heard in the voice of his friend a profound call that would shape not only his life but also the lives of many others.

In the Beginning

blog entry

May 4, 2012

The Voice and The Message

by David Capes

People often ask what The Voice Bible is like. They will sometimes follow that up with: "is it like The Message?" At that point I
pause to see what is coming next. Do they like The Message or
do they not? It's a fair question. People may think of them as being "like" or "similar." In some ways they are. Both The Voice and
The Message are translations of the Christian Scriptures. I don't
accept the characterization that The Message is a paraphrase
because Eugene Peterson worked from and with the original
languages. When you do that, you are doing a translation. Both
The Voice and The Message render the translation in contemporary language and idiom. Both The Voice and The Message have
a similar mission: to put the Scriptures in the hands of a new
audience, an audience that would not likely pick up and read the
more formal translations.

So, in some ways, The Voice and The Message are alike.

But in other ways—important and fundamental ways—The
Voice is different from The Message.

First, The Voice is not the work of a single, great mind. It
represents the collaboration of writers, scholars, poets, and
musicians. This collaboration took place in a variety of ways—in
person, over the phone, over Skype, over e-mail—but it always
represented a back-and-forth movement between the creative
team, the scholars, and the editors at Thomas Nelson.

Second, The Voice is formatted in ways to connect with our
audience. How the text sits on the page matters when trying to

engage a contemporary reader. Take a look at textbooks published over the last 20 years and you will notice how every page is formatted differently with text, text boxes, and other creative, visual helps to aid the student. The Voice had a great design team who worked hard to ensure that every page invited the reader to keep reading. In particular, the dialogue is formatted in a way which is easy to follow. You know immediately who is speaking to whom. We've described this feature as a screen-play format.

Third, The Voice provides introductions to each book, commentary, and reading plans to help people read through the Bible during the church year. Although The Voice is not a "study Bible," in the technical sense, the notes and commentary provide a variety of helps so people can read the Bible with greater clarity. Some of those notes explain key words and concepts. Others provide background and important cultural connections. Still others are designed simply to offer readers a chance to reflect on the text they are reading.

Fourth, those of us who worked on The Voice wanted to avoid trendy language which would become obsolete within a decade or two. Instead we wanted to translate these sacred texts in contemporary language which would not only carry the weight of the Greek's and Hebrew's meaning but also connect with our audiences for years to come.

Fifth, The Voice is a translation which focuses on the story. Though the Bible consists of 66 different books written and edited by hundreds of people over more than 1000 years, we believe that each writer, each book, each episode bears witness to a single great story of love and redemption. This meta-narrative—as scholars call it—tells an amazing story of how the world has gone terribly wrong and how God the Creator has stepped into history to reclaim and restore it. Each book contributes in one way or another to that greater narrative. While many translations seek to get the words right, we went further. Not only did we seek to get the words right, but we thought it was

7

important to get the story right and to invite people to step into that story as it continues to unfold. The formatting, the supplied words, the commentary, and the translation itself are all in service to that greater story of redemption.

The Scriptures tell of a glorious future of new creation; God is "reconciling" all things through Jesus. We can enter into that now through God's gift of grace. When we do, we will find our place among God's people and our mission as those called out ("the Church") to be agents of reconciliation. . . . [2]

Greg Garrett

In 1997 Chris met Greg Garrett. It is probably more accurate to say the two men were thrown together because of their wives. Both women were pregnant at the time with their first children. Both were interested in organic foods, natural childbirth, and attachment parenting. Their common interests brought the two couples together in Waco, Texas. But the pairing of Greg and Chris at first seemed a bit of a mismatch. Greg, deeply entrenched in a stage of life he describes as "anti-Christian," spent many uncomfortable hours in the presence of this Baptist pastor. But Chris was not a typical Baptist preacher, and over time the two became friends and began to share deeply in each other's lives. More than once Chris reached out to Greg when depression forced him to the edge; each time Chris would gently bring him back from the precipice. A genuine, lasting friendship developed.

When Chris was working on a book about the collapse of the energy giant Enron,[3] he turned to Greg. The book presented a number of technical challenges for Chris, and Greg was willing and able to help. Greg had recently completed two novels himself, and both were in the final stages of publication.[4] Chris and Greg enjoyed writing together so much that it seemed natural for them to collaborate on a new project that would become *The Gospel Reloaded: Exploring Spirituality and Faith in* The Matrix.[5] Greg shares openly that the experience of working on the *Matrix* book with Chris was decisive in leading him back to faith. Despite the hardships, depression, and doubts that had plagued him for years, Greg was once again able to imagine himself as a Christian. The book was very successful. In many ways it launched both Chris and Greg into a national spotlight.

Meanwhile both Chris and Greg were invited into a conversation with editors at Zondervan regarding the New International Version. The feedback Zondervan had received on the NIV was that it was not meeting the needs of eighteen- to thirty-five-year-olds. So Chris and Greg attended a focus group in Houston in the fall of 2003 to discuss their insights into culture and frustrations with the current translations. It seemed to them that Zondervan was ready to do a substantial revision of the NIV, and both Chris and Greg figured they were well positioned to help that project move forward. Ultimately, however, Zondervan decided not to revise the NIV at that time. Still, that experience convinced both Chris and Greg that there was room for a new translation geared toward adults below forty years of age.

The Proposal

Chris worked with his agent, John Eames, and crafted a proposal entitled "The Word: The Divine Utterance of the Creator (Known Historically as the Bible)." It laid out the vision for the project.

> *The Word* is a fresh expression of the timeless narrative known as the Bible. Stories that were told to emerging generations of God's goodness by their grandparents and tribal leaders were later recorded and assembled to form the Christian scriptures. Too often the passion, grit, humor, and beauty has [sic] been lost in the translation process. *The Word seeks to recapture what was lost. . . .*
>
> Translating the Bible has too often been a painstaking process correlating the biblical languages to the English vernacular. But our language changes so rapidly that correlating the nominally correct word often fails to communicate the

9

originally intended meaning. In addition, the Bible is filled with passages intended to inspire, captivate, and depict beauty. The old school of translation most often fails at attempts to communicate beauty, poetry, and story. *The Word* is a collage of compelling narratives, poetry, song, truth, and wisdom. *The Word* will call you to enter the whole story of God with heart, soul, and mind.

Such a unique project demanded a team of writers with unprecedented gifts. The proposal described the original team in this way: "an award-winning fiction writer" (Greg Garrett); "an acclaimed poet" (Scott Cairns); "a pastor renowned for using art and narrative in his preaching and teaching" (Chris Seay); "Greek and Hebrew authorities"; and "biblical scholars." In the end Scott Cairns would not contribute to the project. Initially, he had been slated to work on the book of Psalms, but the team decided to divide the individual psalms among a number of scholars, poets, and musicians. Don Miller, author of *Blue Like Jazz*,[6] was also listed among the creators of *The Word*. Don would contribute to the translation and writing of select Old Testament wisdom books.

These contributors took care of the literary side of the project, but Chris's commitment to the visual arts as a means of communicating the gospel was never far removed. For him the splendor of God's story cannot be captured in words alone; he wanted art and images scattered throughout the trade books and Bible to offer a visual reference and source of meditation for the readers. Though this was not carried through every product in The Voice line, it was part of the initial vision and central to the first book, *The Last Eyewitness*.

Chris knew that for the project to be a success it would need a website so beautifully designed that it would reflect the kind of beauty experienced in the poetry and stories of the Bible. So he turned to Tyndall Wakeham who runs BlackPulp, a small but highly specialized team of web designers in Houston. Tyndall had known Chris for several years. As an elder at Ecclesia Houston, he had seen Chris in action and quickly came to understand the need for the project. After consulting together in 2004, they presented some initial ideas to Frank Couch at World Publishing. Eventually those discussions resulted in the project's website, www.hearthevoice.com.

In addition to being beautifully designed, the website was to be a hub of diverse kinds of content and interactivity. If successful, the website would not only promote the project but also contribute to it as well. In other words, the heart of the project and much of its content would be communicated via the Internet. The website was to provide a space for spiritual dialogue and to generate traffic, that is, draw large numbers of people to the site. It was to be a custom website, designed and built from the ground up with every function based on custom-written code. No other website would have a similar look, feel, or functionality.

It is important to remember that when these discussions were taking place social networking was in its infancy. MySpace was more popular than Facebook. Twitter was unheard of. So Tyndall and his team were truly on the cutting edge of Internet design. The website would have several important functions:

- to provide pages that lay out the basic ideas of the project
- to offer custom-built polls and surveys with real-time graphic displays of the results
- to create an online store so customers can purchase products
- to provide space in forums so users can dialogue with each other on spiritual topics
- to host blogs—written and video—by church leaders, scholars, and invited guests
- to allow users to instant message one another
- to archive and stream short films produced by or in concert with the project
- to archive and stream music generated by the project and affiliated artists without unwanted downloads

In short, the website was to build an online community of seekers and believers.

One of the boldest initiatives Tyndall and his team took on was creating the first web-based multiuser audiovisual chat function in the United States. This would allow leaders to make audiovisual presentations before live audiences and to field questions. It would also allow people to use the website to gather and discuss issues face-to-face. On a number of occasions, writers and scholars used this feature of the website to host their collaborations. Again, all of these functions were designed to make it possible for believers to find community on the Internet around the Scriptures.

Thomas Nelson's contract with BlackPulp lasted five years, from 2005 to 2010. At that time Thomas Nelson took over the web design and web-hosting duties for www.hearthevoice.com. Throughout the project the website has been central to promoting The Voice and taking part in its mission. Thomas Nelson has developed other social media outlets for the project through Facebook and Twitter. These connections with users and friends online have helped the project move forward and find a growing audience.

The Audience

The initial proposal drawn up by John Eames on behalf of Chris Seay and his gifted team of writers, scholars, poets, and storytellers described the potential audience as two major target groups.

First, the project was aimed at readers less than forty years of age who haven't bought into or who are burned out on modern exegetical methods. These would likely be Bible readers who had gravitated toward other translations such as The Message, the New Living Translation, and the TNIV in the past. It was anticipated that these readers would be open to and eager for a new translation. The proposal noted that the word-study approach to Bible study—so popular in the 1980s and 1990s—was declining in preference. In its place an emphasis on the entire story of the Bible made it possible for people without the assistance of trained clergy to grasp it on their own. At the same time, Chris knew that many pastors who were older than forty were looking for help in connecting with their potentially younger congregations. The translation he envisioned would help leaders do just that.

Second, the effort was targeted at new readers who have never ventured between the covers of a Bible. These may be younger believers, new believers, or spiritual seekers who would be more receptive to seeing the Bible as a story rather than a list of propositions. In reading theory there is a category known as the "virgin reader," that is, an individual who comes to a book for the first time. There are questions they have, things they need to know if they wish to read a book for all its worth. The translation itself, supplied words, sidebars, notes, formatting, and other features in the proposed products would be designed to help first-time readers understand and step into the story.

In the final analysis what was important to Chris and all those who had come alongside him on this project was the hope that those who picked up The Voice and read it would fall in love with Jesus and come away with a fresh sense of what God was saying to them.

chapter
2

The Development Team

If Chris Seay's vision for a new kind of Bible translation was to be realized, he would need a strong team of gifted men and women to help make it so. Chris is a busy pastor with a growing church. He keeps an active schedule traveling to conferences and networking with Christian leaders across the world. He is a catalytic personality, but he knows his limits and that he does not have enough time or energy to make a major translation happen on his own. So as the vision became clearer, he began to round up a number of people—an agent, a publisher, scholars, assistants, poets, and writers. An early list of contributors included:

- Chris Seay, pastor and writer
- Greg Garrett, fiction writer
- Scott Cairns, poet
- Phuc Luu, Vietnamese pastor and poet
- Justin Hyde, writer and research assistant to Chris Seay

Though Chris knew there could be a large pool of potential contributors to draw from, he wanted to keep the team small enough to be a cohesive voice. He expected the team to change as the project unfolded, and it did. Initially he wanted to limit the contributions of scholars. On December 23, 2003, he wrote to John Eames, "The language and scholarly people will have a limited scope (tell us when we are way off track and add feedback that will help the writers with narrative and details)." Put another way, the scholars were to serve as a kind of tether to make sure the translation remained true to the original voices of the biblical writers. Over time, however, it became clear that scholars must take a larger role in the project.

In all, 120 people contributed in one way or another to this project. Their names are listed at Hearthevoice.com. While small teams of writers and scholars worked through the individual books, a select group of editors and scholars carefully reviewed and, at times, reworked the final rendering. This editorial review committee read each section many times. Other translations give credit to the contributors in a variety of ways, from not identifying any of the contributors to crediting only the final review committee to indicating who worked on what particular book. We make the list of contributors available, but we put the emphasis on the collaborative effort since many different people worked on each book during the different phases of the project.

There are a few people who have been with the project from the beginning or whose contributions to The Voice can hardly be classified or enumerated. In and of themselves, they have some amazing stories. To understand The Voice, you need to know something about them.

John Eames

When the idea for The Voice came to Chris Seay, he knew he would need someone at his side who had extensive experience in publishing. Though Chris had published other books, he recognized that the creation and publication of a new Bible translation was of a different order altogether. In 2003 he met John Eames at the Seattle Film Festival. John knew of Chris from some of his earlier books and wanted to meet him, so John invited Chris to dinner at McCormick and Schmick's not knowing exactly the kind of project Chris had in mind.

John grew up in the northeast and began his career in banking. In 1974 he became aware of a start-up company in Colorado Springs, Colorado, that became NavPress Publishing Group. John sensed it was time to bring his business expertise and acumen into the publishing world. One of the most significant projects John shepherded during his time at NavPress was Eugene Peterson's version of the Bible known as *The Message: The Bible in Contemporary Language.* The Message was published in sections over a nine-year period beginning with the New Testament in 1993. The entire Bible was released in 2002. In many ways The Message blazed a trail for Bible translations and inspired Chris to pursue a new version shaped by a team of artists, writers, and scholars. John Eames's knowledge based on his work with Eugene Petersen in publishing The Message commended him to Chris as the best possible agent for this project.

John worked as the publisher of NavPress for twenty-two years. Then in 1998 he moved to Nashville and lent his publishing experience to the Bible group at Thomas Nelson. Only a few years later, he left behind corporate life to work more personally with authors guiding and representing them to various publishing agencies.

Over dinner that night in Seattle, Chris confided in John about the project. John listened to the idea and felt it did indeed have merit. No recent Bible, John thought, had brought together literary and scholarly talents to tell the story of Scripture and recapture the original voices of the biblical writers. So John agreed to represent Chris and the project.

The job of a literary agent is twofold: (1) to sell an author to a publisher, and (2) to sell the author's proposal. John sensed the first part would be easy since Chris had already established himself as a writer and an innovative church leader. The second part, he thought, would be more difficult because of the scope and expense involved in a project such as translating the Bible. Working with Chris, John created a proposal and began to meet with various publishers.

As John reflects on the last decade and his work with The Voice, it is clear that Thomas Nelson is the right publisher for this version, mostly because of Frank Couch. John describes him as "a Bible guy from way, way, way back." Frank knows Bibles, and he knows those who publish them. During a difficult decade for the publishing industry—as Thomas Nelson faced wrenching problems, large layoffs, acquisition by a private equity firm, among other challenges—the dedication of the company to the project can be attributed to Frank Couch. John Eames has said, "Had it not been for Frank Couch, The Voice Bible would have never seen the light of day."[1]

Frank Couch

Chris Seay met Frank Couch in late January 2004 in Indianapolis at the Christian Bookseller Advance Meeting. By the time Chris and his agent, John Eames, sat down to dinner with Frank, the pair had pitched the idea of a new translation to eight publishers. Little did they know that Frank's entire life had been preparing him to take on this project.

At the time Frank was serving as the editor of World Publishing, a division of Thomas Nelson, acquired when Riverside Book and Bible Distributors sold the business to Thomas Nelson in November 2003. After the acquisition Sam Moore, president of Nelson, brought Frank in to run the editorial side of the business. A few years earlier Sam had approached Frank about his desire to do a new Bible translation based on the critical text. So the idea was already firmly planted in Frank's mind.

The dinner meeting had been arranged by Ted Squires, the vice president for Ministry Resources and World Publishing. At the time Frank was not aware of Chris and his ministry, but he did know John Eames because of their close ties to the publishing industry. Still, when Chris began to speak about the vision he had for a new kind of translation and when he expressed his deep, pastoral concerns for people aged eighteen to thirty-five, Frank recognized a kindred spirit.

Unlike other Bible publishers, Frank had not come from a Christian background. His air force family moved often and seldom attended church. Like many young people today, his family had rejected the church even if they had not completely rejected the idea of God or spiritual things. It was just not something they talked about.

Frank recalls hearing the claims of Christ for the first time in his teenage years the week after President Kennedy was assassinated in 1963. He and his family were living in Germany at the time during the height of the Cold War. Initially the president's death was thought to be a communist plot and so the military began gearing up for war. Europe was shut down; it seemed the world as they knew it was coming apart. Despite the chaos of those days—or perhaps precisely because of it—Frank heard for the first time that Jesus was the Son of God at a Young Life event in Berlin. If he had ever heard that before, it had not registered with him. For some reason, now, at this time, God's Spirit was moving in him. In that moment he prayed that God would begin to reveal to him the truth of the gospel. Six months later, on a ski trip in Switzerland sponsored by Young Life, he became a Christian.

On that same day Frank's sister, Frances, gave him a copy of the J. B. Phillips New Testament. As he read from it, he began to experience God in fresh and meaningful ways. Although he did not understand how the Bible was put together—he became frustrated, for example, that after reading Matthew, Mark basically started over—he nevertheless persevered and continued to read and encounter Christ in its pages. That Phillips New Testament became his prized possession. In the next two years, he would read it cover to cover six times. He remembers carrying this pocket-sized version of the Scriptures with him everywhere he went for the next ten years. So began Frank's love of the Bible.

Frank's family returned to the states for his senior year in high school. With no Young Life program to attend or spiritual community to connect with, Frank recalls it being a rough year. He enrolled at the University of South Florida in Tampa to study physics, but as God's call was becoming clearer to him, he changed his focus to speech communications, with an emphasis in oral interpretation. In his sophomore year he became the student mobilization leader for

Campus Crusade on campus. So began Frank's love of creativity, art, and drama.

Frank thought that he should attend Union Seminary in New York City because it had the only program in religious drama in the country. A late-night call from his pastor, Dick Williams, and the Spirit's gentle prompting changed his mind, and Frank headed west to Dallas Theological Seminary instead. During his second semester, he met Karen, who later became his wife.

After studying for two years in Dallas, Frank was apparently destined to meet Jack Sparks who was on campus recruiting students for ministries with Campus Crusade. Late one afternoon, just minutes before Jack was to leave campus, Frank found him and told him he wanted to use his gifts in drama to share the good news. Jack pointed his finger right in Frank's face and said, "I've been looking for you for over two years."

Frank sensed in these moments a divine appointment, so he and his wife packed up and moved to Berkley, California, where Jack and Pat Matriciano were leaders of the Christian World Liberation Front (CWLF). Frank founded the Berkley Street Theater through which he and others wrote and performed original plays on the streets in Berkley at the height of the countercultural movement. CWLF founded a dance company, distributed food, and sponsored a ranch in Northern California that helped young people get off of drugs. They published leaflets and flyers underground. The content of their plays and publications were never overtly religious, but they did engage the questions and concerns of those who had grown dissatisfied with the status quo. The organizations they founded were about the only ongoing efforts in the country engaging the intellectuals in the countercultural movement. Simply by caring about the things that concerned the people on the streets of Berkley, Frank and his team earned one opportunity after another to share the gospel with people. So began Frank's deep connection with the counterculture, a connection that has never left him.

Frank recalls his first exposure to translation work when Jack

Sparks and a coworker rendered the letters of Paul in street language. His publication, *Letters to Street Christians*, was well received by those who would not likely pick up the King James Bible. The language in the street version was a bit rough, but many young people actually read it and benefited from it.

Eighteen months later Frank and his wife, Karen, moved back to Florida to serve on the staff of Christ Community Church in Tampa, Florida. Frank had been the first person baptized there, and now he was the first staff member, other than the pastor. After serving there, they moved to Tennessee to reconnect with his family. As Frank continued to do drama in churches, he came to the attention of the leadership of Thomas Nelson. Thomas Nelson was about to publish the New King James Version, and Nelson needed a reference system unlike any other. Working as a contractor, it took Frank and his wife, Karen, nine months and three thousand typed pages to create a reference system, which is still used in Thomas Nelson's KJV and NKJV Bibles. Frank's work was so well received he started full-time with Nelson in 1980 as an editor for Bibles. Over the years he has edited nine study Bibles and creatively designed fourteen. In addition to creating the reference system for the NKJV, Frank also worked with Dr. Arthur Farstad to create the textual reference system used in the NKJV. Frank has been part of the launch of three Bible translations prior to The Voice: the New King James, the New Revised Standard, and the Contemporary English Version. So began Frank's long and distinguished career in publishing Bibles for Thomas Nelson.

Frank's life and career have taken a few other twists and turns as lives tend to do. He went back and finished his master's degree at Dallas Theological Seminary. He worked for a time with Lyman Coleman as the president of Serendipity House Publishing. He served as the vice president of Emmaus Bible College in Iowa. He spent some time with Lifeway Christian Resources. But Frank, it seems, always kept circling back to Thomas Nelson. So when Sam Moore called Frank and asked him to come and handle the editorial needs of World Publishing, it wasn't a hard decision.

When Frank left dinner that night with Chris and John in Indianapolis, he knew he had made a new friend in Chris Seay. He knew, too, that before long he would be working with Chris and the rest of the team on a project that fit him like a glove. It was all coming together: his love of Scripture, his gifts in drama and creativity, his ongoing sense of dissatisfaction with culture and connection with the counterculture, and his distinguished career in publishing Bibles. All these strands were coming together in The Voice project. As Frank drove back to Nashville that night through an ice storm, he sensed it was not going to be easy, but it would be worth it.

blog entry

The Most Interesting Man in the World

by David Capes

I've been mildly amused over the last few years by a series of commercials on television. You've probably seen them. They describe "the most interesting man in the world." Here are some of my favorite lines:

> "He has inside jokes with complete strangers."
> "Both sides of his pillow are cool."
> "His mother has a tattoo that reads 'SON.'"
> "At museums he is allowed to touch the art."
> "He is . . . the most interesting man in the world."

This "most interesting man" is, of course, a fictive character invented by clever advertisers trying to sell a Mexican brew. But I think I have met the most interesting man in the world. Not the fictive one, the real one. His name is Frank Couch. Not only have I met him, but I've had the privilege to labor alongside him in The Voice project for over 7 years.

As we have worked together, shared meals together, and traveled together in creating the Voice products and now finally the full Voice Bible, we have had a lot of great conversations. I've been amazed at the places Frank has lived, the sites he has traveled, the people with whom he has worked, the things he knows on a vast range of subjects, and all he has accomplished in his career as a publisher, teacher, and Christian leader. He is a truly amazing fellow. Despite all of that, he is a humble man too.

In the front of The Voice Bible James F. [Frank] Couch Jr. is listed as one of 11 people involved in "Editorial Review." That tells about 1/1000th of the story. Frank was the executive editor of the project. In other words he ate, slept, and drank The Voice for 7 years. He did that even as he managed and took care of hundreds of other Thomas Nelson–related issues. I don't know how he did it, but I do know he immersed himself totally in the project. He wrote, rewrote, edited, reedited, corrected, reviewed, and managed the hundred something people who worked at every level of the project. John Eames of Eames Literary Services in Nashville is correct when he noted to me recently: this project would have never seen the light of day without Frank Couch.

In 1 Corinthians 11:1 Paul writes: "So imitate me, *watch my ways, follow my example,* just as I, too, *always seek to* imitate the Anointed One." Paul knows that believers need flesh and blood examples after whom to pattern their lives. So Jesus' emissary set himself up as that example. If the Corinthians watch Paul, they will see Jesus. If they imitate Paul, they will become like Jesus. Whether we realize it or not, key aspects of our lives are formed as we watch, admire, and pattern our lives after one another. It happens naturally, almost unconsciously. We must be careful the kind of people we choose to follow. If we pay attention, we will notice God placing along our path men and women worthy of imitation. For me and hundreds of other people, Frank is that sort of man. That makes him extremely interesting and important in God's Kingdom.

I hope that someday Frank will write his story or get someone else to do it, because I think most people would be astounded and inspired by his life. I know I am.

As you read The Voice Bible, give thanks to God for the extraordinary life, talents, and experience of Frank Couch.[2]

Maleah Bell

Maleah Bell has been in church all of her life. Her father was a deacon in the Baptist church, and Maleah earned all the proper pins for attendance in Sunday school. With that kind of pedigree, it was probably inevitable that she would marry a pastor who serves a Baptist church in Middle Tennessee. In a real sense Maleah's heart and mind were perfectly prepared to reflect how the people in the pew might think of a new Bible translation. The Voice project was an eye-opening experience for Maleah; she was surprised to encounter so many people who were turned off by traditional churches but still desired to connect to authentic Christian communities.

Maleah first met Frank Couch in the 1980s when they were both employed at Thomas Nelson. After ten years at Nelson, she left the company to raise her children and accompany her husband, Greg, to Fort Worth, Texas, where he attended Southwestern Baptist Theological Seminary. After his graduation, Greg pastored a church in Alabama, and eventually, the Bells returned to Nashville to accept a pastorate there. Shortly thereafter, Maleah joined Frank at World Publishing.

Even on the publishing side, Maleah was no stranger to Bibles. She worked for several years with Frank at World Publishing where they published several study Bibles. Now at Thomas Nelson, she was the associate editor on The Voice project, which officially meant she assisted Frank in managing the hundred-plus writers and scholars—not always the easiest people to manage—and editing thousands of files. In the end, Maleah did far more for the project than can be expressed in a title. She worked and shaped nearly every part of it.

Among other things Maleah was responsible for coordinating and reviewing all editorial work. When questions arose regarding a particular translation or commentary, she turned to either Frank Couch or David Capes for answers. Because of her pleasant demeanor, Maleah was a good friend to the scholars and writers; and because of her hint of southern sass, she kept everyone in line.

Toward the middle of the project, her duties were expanded. Maleah reviewed all the words placed in italic type to ensure the accuracy and clarity of the text. The italicized type represents words that (a) are not tied directly to the translations from the original languages and (b) are supplied to assist the reader in understanding the text. The use of italicized words in Bible translations has become standard practice in Bible publishing. A glance at the King James Version or New American Standard Bible demonstrates the practice is widespread. In The Voice, however, the editorial team provided more supplied words because the intended audience was expected to have little or no knowledge of the Bible before they started reading. In the past, Bible publishers had the luxury of expecting a high level of biblical literacy from their readers; today that luxury exists only in small pockets.

For Maleah The Voice was more than a job; it was a calling. One day when Dr. Jay Strack, president of Student Leadership University, was visiting the Thomas Nelson headquarters in Nashville, he turned to Maleah and said, "Take good care of The Voice, Maleah." These words stuck with her and shaped her attitude throughout the rest of the project. She thought often about the responsibility she carried as a key member of the editorial team toiling to bring this new Bible translation to print. Everyone who knows Maleah could see The Voice was in good hands.

For seven years she worked almost exclusively on The Voice; for three of those years she worked from home. The home environment offered her a quiet and contemplative place to work. She was able to focus her attention and make good progress, but the downside for Maleah was that she grew tired of being alone. At times she missed the face-to-face interaction. Still Maleah is a woman of great faith; she sensed God's presence with her throughout the project. By the end of the project, she had read through the Bible several times. She jokes, "If the church gave an award for daily Bible reading, nobody could touch me. I'd win, hands down."

Merrie Noland

When Frank Couch and Maleah Bell needed help with The Voice, they turned to Merrie Noland. Merrie was the senior editor for Bibles with Thomas Nelson. She worked with the company for thirty years. Though Merrie had a quiet side—a must for any editor—she was also a lot of fun. It was Merrie's job to take an approved file, read it with a fresh set of eyes for any issues that might have been missed, and then send the file on to typesetting. Most of Merrie's input into the production of the books was accomplished late in the process, which meant her changes usually made it to publication.

Merrie died suddenly on May 11, 2011, only a few months before the full Bible was finished and published. Even though she had been undergoing cancer treatments, she continued to work day after day on The Voice and other Nelson products. Still her body could not stand the onslaught of the disease and its treatment.

Merrie enjoyed working on The Voice right up to the end of her life. Ironically, the last book she proofread and edited was the book of Genesis, the book of beginnings. One of Merrie's important contributions came at this stage in the project when she started recasting all the essays into present tense. This simple change makes the text and commentary seem more alive and came from Merrie's inner sense of what was best for the new translation. You see, she understood well The Voice project. She wanted to help us celebrate the fact that God has spoken in the past and He is speaking now through these amazing books of the Bible. Merrie desired for us to hear the voice of God now in our lives. Frank Couch, the executive editor, liked the changes Merrie was making to the essays and continued to use the present tense globally through the rest of the commentary.

When Merrie died suddenly, Frank and Maleah turned to Misty Bourne and Matt Burleson to continue the important work Merrie started. Misty knew what big shoes she had to fill.

blog entry

November 21, 2011

Remembering Merrie

By Misty Bourne

The day the text of The Voice was finally ready to go to the printer, we had quite a commotion in our corner of the building. There were tears, laughter, and even (dare I confess?) a little dancing! Seven years of laborious efforts were coming to a close for our internal editor on the project, the only one in the building that day who had worked on it for so long. I cried with her, even though I had only worked on The Voice for a few months.

The air was charged with so many thoughts—thoughts of victory, uncertainty, satisfaction, relief—that it was hard to discern who was feeling what and why. Now that it's been a few days since we sent the text files off to the printer, I've had some time to think through the powerful feelings that overwhelmed me that day.

When I reflect on the project, I feel overcome with humility. I was never supposed to work on The Voice. My sweet friend, Merrie Noland, was going to coordinate the proofreading. She was an amazing woman and an extremely knowledgeable editor who had been with Thomas Nelson for more than thirty years. I always looked up to her for her skill, her attitude and her perseverance. And what seemed like in a flash, she was gone—she passed away this past summer after a battle with cancer. I was honored to be asked to work on The Voice simply because of Merrie's legacy, because of her talent and her spirit. I could never hold a candle to Merrie, but I'm proud to have carried a project through in her stead.

Simultaneously, I feel extremely grateful to Frank Couch (Vice President for Translation Development) and Maleah Bell (Associate Editor), who asked me to work on The Voice. I'm thankful that they trust me and believe in me enough to put such an important project in my hands. More than that, I'm grateful to and humbled by God that He would bless me with the gift of working on a new Bible translation, a translation that I believe will change people's lives. Who am I to work on His Word? I've always felt it a privilege to work on the Bible, but that feeling is much stronger now than it's ever been.

As our group journeys into this next phase, spreading the Word and sharing The Voice, I echo Paul's words to the Romans and pray for the success of this product and the inspiring of many lives for God:

> So to the One who is able to strengthen you to live consistently with my good news and the preaching of Jesus, the Anointed, with the revelation of the ancient mystery that has been kept secret since the earliest days, this mystery is revealed through the prophetic voices passed down in the Scriptures, as they have been commanded by the Eternal God. In this time, this mystery is being made known to the nations so that all may be led to faith-filled obedience. To the one true and wise God, we offer glory for all times through Jesus, the Anointed One. Amen (Romans 16:25–27).[3]

Amanda Haley

Amanda will be the first one to tell you that God has guided her life in spite of her best efforts. She sensed a call to ministry in her teenage years, but she couldn't reconcile that calling with the limited ministry opportunities she saw for women in her church. Determined to shake the feeling, she enrolled at Rhodes College in Memphis, Tennessee, as an international law major but soon found herself gravitating toward courses in religion. She fell in love with biblical archaeology and changed her major to religion with a minor in Middle Eastern studies. Mentors at Rhodes convinced her to continue her academic study of the Bible at Harvard Divinity School. She earned a master's degree in Hebrew Scripture and Interpretation.

Amanda and her husband, David, rushed back home to Middle Tennessee the week after she graduated with no jobs and no real plan. They loved Massachusetts, but couldn't afford even one more month's rent. Amanda thought she'd take a year off of school and then apply to doctoral programs, maybe teach a children's Sunday school class. That year was supposed to be a pause button in her life, but one month after the move she met someone at church named Frank Couch who spotted her talents and immediately hired her to proof Bibles for World Publishing. A month later Frank introduced Amanda to Chris Seay and Kelly Hall in Nashville. When Chris shared with Amanda about the project, he sensed that she understood it; so he invited her to become the main translator of 1 and 2 Chronicles for Ecclesia Bible Society.

Amanda's duties grew quickly from there, on both the publishing and the writing sides. She began to work as a freelancer copyediting the New Testament and contributing to some of the book introductions. Amanda went on to translate the book of Ezra as well as to rework other historical books such as 1 and 2 Samuel and 1 and 2 Kings. She also contributed to some Old Testament commentary. When that was complete, she turned her attention to the biblical review of the entire Old Testament. As executive editor, Frank wanted to make sure that The Voice translation was not too dependent on other published works. It is easy for a favorite version or turn of phrase to stick in the mind of translators as they are working through passages. Amanda was charged to make sure that The Voice translators and reviewers had not reproduced other readings unknowingly.

When Amanda thinks about the finished product, she says that

The Voice is much closer to the original languages than she initially thought it would be. The care exercised by the writers, scholars, and editorial team kept The Voice true to the Hebrew, Greek, and Aramaic. Amanda is thankful that God didn't let her pause her life and called her to be a part of a finished translation that meets academic standards but is not stiff and hard to read. It presents the Scriptures in its proper historical and literary contexts, and as she loves to say to the adults she now teaches at church, "Context is everything."

David Capes

When Chris Seay needed an academic to work with Ecclesia Bible Society in order to guide and manage the contributions of scholars to the project, he turned to Dr. David Capes, professor of New Testament at Houston Baptist University. Two years earlier David and his family joined Ecclesia Houston because he sensed something unique and important was happening with this community. Little did he know The Voice project was in his immediate future.

When the project got off the ground, David had taught Greek and New Testament for fourteen years at Houston Baptist University. He had also served as adjunct faculty for Austin Presbyterian Theological Seminary and later Fuller Seminary in Houston. He was the author of three books and numerous articles on themes primarily related to the New Testament. But the crucial quality he brought to Ecclesia Bible Society was the network he had through the Society of Biblical Literature and the Institute for Biblical Research. Those connections to schools and scholars would prove useful as they began to seek qualified contributions to the project.

David served as one of the primary translators, reviewers, and writers on the project on behalf of Ecclesia Bible Society. He was also tasked with finding scholars willing to contribute to the project. In that he faced several challenges. First, many religion scholars do not have the skills necessary to engage in a sustained effort to translate the entire Bible. Second, scholars who can translate from the biblical languages and/or review the work of others either were already involved in other translation projects or had recently completed another translation project. It is often the case that those who contribute to a new version of the Bible are hesitant to do it again because the process is long and demanding. Furthermore, since translators are working as a team, frequently their suggestions are not incorporated into the final, printed version. Some scholars, it seems, have a rather low tolerance for that kind of disappointment. Third, other scholars were just too busy on their own research agendas to be able to meet the aggressive deadlines set up by Ecclesia Bible Society and Thomas Nelson. Initially, the plan called for the project to be completed in four years. To make that happen, scholars would have to set aside their own research for the sake of The Voice. Not many scholars are willing to do that. Fourth, still other academics had a difficult time understanding the project. They might know how scholars collaborate with each other in a translation effort, but they could not imagine how collaboration with writers, poets, and artists might work. Academics are often reluctant to be involved in projects in which they are not in control.

The scholars invited to contribute to the project represented a range of denominations and theological interests, but all were committed to the church. Chris and David wanted some academics on the team who were well-published and therefore well-known; but they also wanted lesser-known people to contribute because often the scholarly guilds only privilege a few select voices. It is too often the case that when a project begins, they simply "round up the usual suspects," and the same people contribute over and over. Clearly, there are other capable scholars in colleges, universities, and seminaries who can and should be contributing to this kind of effort; it was incumbent upon David to find them and bring them into the fold. It was also important for him to bring to the conversation some of the younger, newer voices. Though this was not to be a translation by scholars for scholars, it was crucial to make sure The Voice was informed by the latest advances in biblical studies. The best way to do that was to invite younger scholars to join the effort.

Later in the project, Frank Couch realized that David's skills and interests in the project could be useful in working from the publisher's side as well. Still, a heavy teaching schedule and administrative duties at the university made that difficult, so Frank arranged for Thomas Nelson to buy out some of David's teaching time so he could devote more time to the project. That arrangement eventually led Thomas Nelson and HBU to partner in naming Dr. Capes the Thomas Nelson Research Professor at HBU. This unique collaboration between a major publisher and a university made it possible for David to continue teaching and to give the majority of his time to completing the translation and representing it to the public.

Kelly Hall

Kelly Hall's spiritual journey has taken a number of twists and turns. Though she was baptized Catholic, her family stopped attending when she was a child. At nineteen she met Mark who was also raised Catholic but was questioning faith. When they agreed to marry in 1996, Kelly completed confirmation classes both to please her mother-in-law and to be married in the same church as her parents had been married.

Kelly has always had a connection with nature. She describes her experience of creation as deeply mystical and spiritual. Her interest in developing a healthy, nature-centered lifestyle connected her with people with similar interests, and she and Mark signed up for basic Wiccan classes at a midtown Houston store. Through these classes they met and made friends with the high priest and priestess of a coven, and one day they were invited to join. Neither Kelly nor Mark understood exactly what it meant to be in a coven; she admits to being a bit naive at the time, but they had few friends outside the family, and it felt good to be invited into the community to express their spirituality. One night at a campout, however, as strange rituals were taking place around them, it dawned on Kelly and Mark that they were in the wrong place. All they wanted to do was to get back to nature, to live according to the natural order of things, and to see people as part of that natural order. The next morning they decided to leave the campout and the coven. When coven officials became aware of their intentions, they instructed them to sever ties with the group by burning any and all items associated with it.

Meanwhile Kelly and Mark enrolled their oldest child into Waldorf School in Houston. While there Kelly seemed to be embarking on a new chance for community. One of the parents at the school was a pastor at an urban church; he invited the Hall family to visit his church sometime. Terrified, Kelly politely said, "Maybe so," and left it at that. Being on the outside of Christianity for so long made her fear the name "Jesus." One day in 2003, after long, intense bouts of depression, Kelly announced, "I'm going to church." Stunned, Mark responded, "I'm going with you."

The pastor who initially invited the Halls to church was, of course, Chris Seay. Kelly and Mark began to sense that God was calling them to enter into a new relationship through Jesus, and Chris's church, Ecclesia Houston, would become their community of faith. They said yes to the call and soon found their place in God's family. Not long after Kelly and her family began attending Ecclesia Houston, Chris spoke on the parable of the talents and offered seed money to the congregation for anyone who would take and multiply it to help raise funds toward building maintenance. Inspired by the message, Kelly decided to take the money and self-publish a book of her poems. *From Dark Places to Heavenly Spaces* was largely about what it felt like to be imprisoned by depression and set on the pathway to healing.

Chris and Lisa Seay became a large part of Kelly's support. Because their children went to the same school, Chris noticed that Kelly was quick to volunteer and help organize events at the small, start-up school. One night as she was considering becoming a teacher, Chris invited her to join Ecclesia Bible Society and The Voice team. Although the project was well underway when Kelly agreed, she soon found herself at the center of a dynamic venture carrying out a number of crucial functions.

Initially Kelly assisted Chris in managing the project. She worked as a liaison between Ecclesia Bible Society in Houston and Thomas Nelson in Nashville. While Chris made the decisions regarding scholars and writers, Kelly carried out those decisions on his behalf. She handled the contracts, payments, and requisite tax documents. She tracked the manuscripts that streamed through cyberspace between scholars, writers, reviewers, and editors. She also kept track of the writers' and scholars' progress. As scholars and writers fell behind, she gently prodded them and urged them to get the work in.

The team worked out a flowchart for how the translation process should work, and they placed a black arrow between the different contributors like this: scholar → writer → reviewer, etc. In all there were fourteen levels of writing and review. Here is where Kelly came in. She was the black arrow. Every time a person finished a file, it was sent to Kelly. It was Kelly's job to make sure it was properly tagged, keep a copy of it, and send it on to the next person for review, rewriting, editing, proofreading, or acceptance. This happened thousands and thousands of times. Kelly "Black Arrow," as she was often called, served a crucial function in bringing the manuscript to publication.[4]

Eventually Kelly's writing skills came into play. In October 2005, as Chris was going through the scholarly review process for John's Gospel, one of his best friends, Kyle Lake, was electrocuted after stepping into the water to baptize at University Baptist Church in Waco, Texas. A lethal jolt of electricity ended the young pastor's life before anyone else stepped into the water. With deadlines looming, Chris relied on Kelly to help make editorial changes and keep the project moving for its first release, *The Last Eyewitness*. Moved by the beauty of its story, as well as by the collaboration of The Voice team, Kelly composed a poem that is published in the front of the book. As she proved willing and able to handle the text, Chris invited her to work on select psalms and proverbs. Kelly brought a light touch and poetic sensitivity to every verse and phrase she considered. She also teamed up with Chris and others to translate through the thirteen letters attributed to Paul. The emissary's letters can be heavy at times, but there are chapters and verses that resonate with beauty and poetry as well.

Meanwhile Frank Couch, too, could see how dedicated Kelly was to the project. She was a delight to work with and eager to help. Though she was hired by Thomas Nelson to work on behalf of Ecclesia Bible Society, Frank knew he could use her editorial and proofreading skills on the Thomas Nelson side of the process. Before long, Kelly was lending a hand to Frank and Maleah in copyediting, proofing, and fine-tuning the manuscripts for publication.

There were many other men and women who contributed significantly to The Voice, but it was these six people, who along with Chris Seay and Greg Garrett, who did the most to shape the project.

chapter
3

The Version Title

When Chris Seay met with John Eames in 2004, the vision and name for the project were still taking shape. Chris wanted to create a new category for Bibles other than paraphrase or translation. He felt the categories were themselves misunderstood and failed to provide the clarity needed to describe what he hoped to accomplish with this project. As a pastor he was interested primarily in proclamation. Other translations, he found, did not lend themselves to preaching to the kind of people assembling to hear him open the Scriptures week after week. Whatever this new Bible version would be, it must be useful in preaching and it must be beautiful and compelling when read aloud.

In those early days Chris often used the word *retelling* to describe the method and results. He hoped to retell the biblical stories in ways that are contemporary, ancient, literary, challenging, and beautiful. He was convinced that people connect with stories and storytelling rather than the recitation of isolated facts. Jesus, of course, taught through stories, parables, and metaphors; but modern Christians have reduced his teaching to a system of irrefutable facts. This is why Chris wanted to bring together writers, scholars, poets, and storytellers to bring the Scripture to life in ways that celebrate both their truth and their beauty.

The proposal created by Eames Literary Services of Nashville,

Tennessee, and circulated to potential publishers in February 2004 was entitled "The Word: The Divine Utterance of The Creator (Known Historically as the Bible)." The contributors of the project were proposed, "As Translated, Edited, and Illustrated by Chris Seay and a gifted team of Writers, Scholars, Poets, and Story Tellers." The proposal laid out the vision, audience, and creators of The Word. It offered some endorsements, potential related products, and initial marketing and promotional ideas.

But even as the method, the vision, and even some of the marketing ideas were becoming clear, the title for this project was still unclear. In March 2004 Chris Seay, Greg Garrett, Frank Couch, Ramona Richards, and Dan Mann met to discuss the project name and other topics. Greg Garrett recalls,

> As I tend to do in meetings, I let my thoughts drift. I was thinking about the voice speaking creation into being in Genesis 1—certainly one of the seminal moments in the Bible—and that sparked some thought about the prologue in John: what if we thought of the Word as that Voice, speaking creation into being? For me, that linked up creation in the Hebrew Testament with creation in the Christian Testament in a really dynamic way.[1]

But when and how did Greg first start thinking of "the voice" as a generative theme for the project? Frank Couch recollects that early in the discussions he made a statement about how important it is to recover the voices of the individual biblical writers. Exactly who expressed the idea first and how that happened is beyond anyone's clear recollection. Most likely it was in the meeting of the minds that these ideas surfaced for the first time. Still when it was voiced, everyone present sensed they may be onto something. Now "The Voice" was on the table. At that point there were three main contenders: "The Word," "The Story of God," and "The Voice."

37

Later that year Chris sent an e-mail to potential contributors in which he laid out over forty potential names for the project. After some feedback from those contributors, these five were the most chosen:

1. The Emerging Voice: An Artistic Retelling of the Christian Scriptures
2. The Word: A Divine Utterance of the Creator Known Historically as The Bible
3. Listen! The Voice Speaks, and Makes All Things New
4. The Voice: Re-telling the Biblical Narrative
5. VOX: Retelling the Biblical Narrative

From this list it is obvious that the team was gravitating toward the imagery of "The Voice." Even the title "The Word" was subtitled "A Divine Utterance," which implies divine speech. Prompted by his conversations with Greg, Chris began to see that "The Voice," properly understood, was a helpful and imaginative way to nuance the meaning of the *Logos* in John 1.

The *Logos*—John 1:1

Nearly all English translations of John 1:1 are word for word the same: "In the beginning was the Word, and the Word was with God, and the Word was God" (KJV). Of the major translations the only outlier is the New Living Translation: "In the beginning the Word already existed. The Word was with God, and the Word was God." These are accurate translations of the first verse of John's prologue. But the question remains, is the translation clear? For Chris the issue centered on the meaning of the Greek word *logos*. While the Greek word *logos* can mean "word," it is not the only word or perhaps even the best word to render the meaning of John 1:1 for a modern audience.

The Arndt-Gingrich-Danker New Testament Lexicon, a standard reference work, gives over twenty options for translating *logos*, all of which appear in the New Testament. Here are just some of the ways the New American Standard Bible, often considered one of the most literal translations, translates *logos*:

- word (Matthew 12:32)
- matter under discussion (Mark 8:32)
- statement (Matthew 5:37)
- story (Matthew 28:15)
- message (Luke 4:32)
- saying (John 21:23)
- thing (Matthew 21:24)
- news (Mark 1:45)
- report (Luke 7:17)
- question (Mark 11:29)
- complaint (Acts 19:38)
- account (Matthew 18:23; Acts 1:1)
- reason (Matthew 5:32)[2]

Clearly, the semantic field of *logos* is broad. Common, however, to most of these definitions is the notion that *logos* has something to do with speaking, types of speech, or that which is said. The Greek verb *legein*, which is cognate to *logos*, means essentially "to speak." This suggests that there may be another way, perhaps a better way for a modern audience to understand *logos* than as "the Word."

One problem in translating *logos* as "word" is the Christian association of *word* with the Bible. Christians often refer to the Scriptures as "the word of God." This has led some to imagine that in John 1:1 the writer was referring to the Bible. But a close reading will reveal that when John referred to the logos, he was not talking about the Bible. As the capitalization of *word* in English translations suggests, it is a title for a divine person. Essentially, as John is recasting the story of creation in his prologue, he is celebrating two new revelations that set the tone for his Gospel: (1) the person and role of the preexistent Jesus in creation, and (2) the conviction that in Jesus God has become flesh and lived among us.

A second and more significant problem regards the intended audience. Veteran readers of the Bible may understand some aspects of what John is trying to convey about the Word only because they have heard multiple sermons or lessons on it. But even then, how deep does their knowledge go? With biblical literacy on the decline, we can no longer be confident that the average Bible reader understands what John meant when referring to Jesus as "the Word." What about the novice Bible readers for whom this translation is intended? When they read, "In the beginning was the Word, and the Word was with God and the Word was God," they may well be left scratching their heads. If they apply any standard definition or meaning to *Word*, they will not grasp much of what John has in mind. It is not enough to suggest as one man did: "If people do not understand what a word in the Bible means, let them ask their pastor." That is exactly the problem. The people we had in mind as our prime audience for this translation do not have pastors or access to commentaries to help them sort out the more weighty theological concepts. Every week stories in the news describe fewer people in the West attending churches. On a regular basis we hear that young people are leaving the church perhaps never to return again. The Voice translation is written to connect with them in every way possible.

The more Chris reflected on John 1, the more he came to see "the Voice" as a useful translation of the apostle's meaning and of an important theme throughout all of Scripture. John's Gospel does not exist in isolation. It is part of a grand story of love and redemption which affirms that since the beginning, God has been speaking. He spoke creation into existence. He spoke to Abraham and created a covenant people. He spoke authoritatively through His servants, the prophets. He spoke finally and definitively in Jesus His Son. In the Scriptures, if we listen carefully, we will hear God speaking and addressing us. In fact, the Greek word *ekklēsia* in the New Testament translated *church* means those who have heard God's call and said yes to that call.

As the team reflected on these ideas—God creating, God speaking, God calling—the word *Voice* continued to come to mind. For this and other reasons, The Voice became the title of this project. In the end it was decided not to render the Greek word *logos* simply by the English *the Voice*:

> In the beginning
>> Before time itself was measured, the Voice [*logos*] was speaking.
>>> The Voice was and is God.
>> This *celestial* Word [*logos*] remained ever present with the
>>> Creator;
>>> His speech shaped the entire cosmos. (John 1:1–3a)

Note, first of all, that these verses are formatted in poetic form. The rhythm and structure of these opening lines to John's prologue suggest they be read as more than prose. As the editorial team sought to capture something of the beauty and meter of these opening verses, it seemed best to cast it in poetic form. Note, second, that *logos* is translated here both as "the Voice" and "the Word." This was done (a) to introduce a new image to help a modern reader appreciate the scope of John's revelation and (b) to pay homage to the traditional renderings wherein Jesus is referred to as "the Word." It is the stacking of the images with all of their rich meanings and associations that helps the reader grasp some of what John means when he refers to Jesus as the *Logos*.

The Voice and Its Associations

The word *voice* has a meaning, but it also carries with it a number of important associations. First, voices are personal. Voices, like fingerprints, are unique and individual. You can tell one person from another simply by his or her voice. Depending on the sophistication of certain voice-recognition software, the program may have to be trained to follow how its user pronounces certain sounds in order to get the transcriptions right. Second, voices are relational. We have all had the experience of hearing from an old friend and saying, "So good to hear your voice." To know a voice is to know something special about a person. To hear a familiar voice is to be taken back to comforting times. Third, voices reveal as much or more than words. The tone of a person's voice exposes what a person is thinking or feeling in ways that transcend the words spoken. Communication specialists are fond of saying that most communication is nonverbal; they tell us to listen more for how something is said than for what specifically is said. Clearly *voice* as it regards to Scripture is capable of important connections and could prove useful in helping people engage the entire story.

While hearing "the voice of God" is an important theme throughout Scripture, there are three passages that have shaped our thinking on the use and theme of *voice*.

The Voice of the Good Shepherd

As John's story unfolds, Jesus is locked in conflict with powerful leaders who try to trick Him publicly and shame Him and His followers into silence (chapters 8–9). In John 10 Jesus offers His disciples an important teaching on His nature and His role as the Good Shepherd (John 10:1–4; boldface added for emphasis).

> Jesus: I tell you the truth: the man who crawls through the fence of the sheep pen, rather than walking through the gate, is a thief or a vandal. The shepherd walks openly through the entrance. The guard who is posted to protect the sheep opens the gate for the shepherd, and **the sheep hear his voice.** He **calls his own sheep** by name and leads them out. When all the sheep have been gathered, he walks on ahead of them; and **they follow him because they know his voice.** The sheep would not be willing to follow a stranger; they run because they do not know the voice of a stranger.

In this parable Jesus employs an evocative image with which His audience could easily identify. Everyone in Jesus' audience had seen a flock of sheep dutifully following its shepherd, called together simply and somewhat mysteriously by the familiar sound of his voice. When the shepherd calls the sheep, it is not the words he uses—for the animals cannot grasp their meaning—it is the sound and tone of his voice that touches something deep within their sheep psyche. On the other hand, they had also seen or heard stories of thieves who could not roust a flock in order to herd it away from its secure pasture. Jesus uses this well-known image to contrast His own role with the attempts of the thieves and vandals to bring harm to the flock.

The imagery Jesus employs is not new to Him or His audience; it is drawn from the voices of the prophets and poets of Israel. Centuries earlier they celebrated the Eternal as their shepherd and Israel as His flock (Psalm 23; Isaiah 40:11). They warned of false shepherds who would come and lead the flock astray (Jeremiah 10:21; Ezekiel 34:2–4). Israel's singers and poets predicted that one day, in the not-too-distant future, a good shepherd would arrive to love and care for God's flock (Jeremiah 23:4–6; Ezekiel 34:23–24). Rather than using the sheep and exploiting them for his own selfish ends (as the wicked shepherds do), the good shepherd will bandage the injured, look for the lost, and unite the flock once again.

In Jesus' parable He speaks of Himself cryptically as a shepherd who arrives by the only legitimate route, the gate of the sheep pen. Recognized by the gatekeeper, as the shepherd calls for his sheep, the gate swings open wide. When they hear the pleasant sound of his familiar voice, they raise their heads and move submissively in sheep-like fashion toward the sound. As they catch their first glimpse of him, their pace quickens and they hurry to surround him. He knows them and calls them by name, and they follow him, once again wooed by the pleasant sound of his voice.

As Jesus teaches His disciples, it seems that some are not fully grasping His meaning; so Jesus zeroes in further. This time He adds another image to the mix. Now He is the gate of the sheep. Thieves and robbers had come before, but the sheep ignored their calls and took no comfort in their voices. Those who enter through Jesus, He says, experience liberation and find true pasture because He came to give them life, abundant and joyful (John 10:6–10).

Jesus returns to His initial teaching with the triumphant: "I am the good shepherd. The good shepherd lays down His life for the sheep *in His care*" (John 10:11). Compared to the hired hands who run away at the first sign of trouble, the good shepherd lays down his life. He knows his sheep, and his sheep know him. At the sound of his voice, the entire flock is united into one flock led by one shepherd.

The Still, Small Voice

One of the episodes in Elijah's life provides a completely different way of thinking about *voice*. The prophet Elijah was flying high when God showed up in a big way to vindicate him before a watching nation at Mount Carmel (1 Kings 18:20–46). But the king and queen were watching too, and they were not happy. The royal couple had embraced gods other than the One True God, so Elijah's victory looked like their defeat. In fact, Queen Jezebel sent him a message telling him he would be dead in the next twenty-four hours if she had anything to say about it.

Elijah's euphoria slipped quickly into depression as the prophet fled for his life. He traveled south to Beersheba. As the depression deepened, he prayed to God that death might relieve his suffering. The consolation of sleep eventually fell upon the terrified prophet. As he rested a special messenger of God appeared and told him to get up and to eat and drink a meal prepared for him. After more rest and another meal, he was told to travel again. He journeyed south and west for forty days and forty nights and arrived at Mount Horeb, the place where God's people Israel received laws from Moses. Elijah was reversing the journey God's covenant people took into the land of promise centuries earlier under the watchful guidance of Moses and Joshua.

Elijah took shelter in a cave and rested for the night (1 Kings 19:1–8). As the prophet stewed over his plight, God showed up again. The Eternal asked Elijah why he was there even as the prophet protested that he alone of all the people and prophets had remained faithful to Israel's God. The Eternal responded by telling the prophet to move outside the cave and stand in his presence. What happened next would redirect Elijah's life. The Eternal passed by and allowed the prophet to experience a series of theophanies.

A theophany occurs when God appears in one form or another to one of His servants. The biblical story contains a number of theophanies. Each appearance (such as those in Exodus 19:16; Isaiah 6:1–4; Ezekiel 1; and Acts 2) is accompanied by powerful phenomena such as thunder, lightning, earthquakes, fire, and wind.

When the Eternal passed by the first time, the winds picked up and became so strong rocks tumbled down the mountain and shattered to pieces. But the prophet could see the Eternal was not in the wind. Then a powerful earthquake rocked the ground beneath his feet. But the prophet could see that God was not in the earthquake. Then fire flashed in the wilderness. But the prophet could see the Eternal was not in the fire. Finally, the prophet heard a different sound, the sound of a "still small voice" (1 Kings 19:12 NKJV). God was not in the earth, the wind, the fire; He was in that still, small voice.

Elijah must have been puzzled. He knew the stories of what happened centuries earlier on this very mountain when Moses went up to meet God and establish the covenant with those recently freed slaves. In those days God's majesty was clearly evident in the earth, wind, and fire. Elijah himself, of course, had seen God come through impressively on Mount Carmel; he reveled in the clear victory of the Eternal over the false gods. Now Elijah needed another kind of lesson: the Eternal is not always and only in the powerful and majestic; sometimes, God speaks in the gentle breezes and the solitude of a quiet voice.

A Voice Like a Roaring Waterfall

When John was exiled on the bleak little island of Patmos, he had a vision of the risen Jesus. As he shared that vision in the book we know as the Revelation with the seven churches of Asia Minor, he framed

45

what he saw in the language he knew best: the language of Scripture. He saw, he said, the Son of Man moving among the seven lampstands, dressed in a long robe, draped in a gold sash, His head and hair pure white. These phrases do more than describe what John saw; they echo the language used by earlier prophets and poets to describe visions they saw as they, too, experienced the glorious presence of God. When John came to describe the voice he heard, he said, "His voice *filled the air and* sounded like a roaring waterfall" (Revelation 1:15). This description comes directly from Ezekiel's vision of God's glory returning to the temple following the exile (Ezekiel 43:2). John said to hear the voice of the risen Jesus is like hearing the voice of God. It sounds like a roaring waterfall (literally, "the sound of many waters").

If you have ever been near a waterfall, then you know something of John's experience. Toccoa Falls in northern Georgia has a vertical drop of 186 feet; it is one of the tallest free-falling waterfalls in the east. If you were to wade into the chilly, mountain waters and slip closer to the base of the falls, not only would you be drenched in the mist, but you would soon find all other sound completely drowned out by the "voice" of the falling waters. You would look around you and see leaves rustling silently in the wind. You would watch as cars and trucks move by on a nearby road without a sound. You would have to shout to make yourself heard to a friend standing only a few feet away. It would be as if all sound gave way to the sound of the falling waters. This is how Ezekiel and John imagined and described the voice of God in their famous visions.

These stories from Scripture informed how the translation team approached this project. If we could truly hear The Voice, it would drown out every other voice in society straining to be heard. Like some heavenly "white noise," it would fill every frequency, mask every sound. At times God does speak in dramatic and powerful ways, but these times are rare. More often God is not in the flashy and power-filled—despite our addictions to glitz, glitter, and power. Elijah learned that at important times God is in the stillness, the gentleness, the calm. If we are to hear it, we need to quiet ourselves.

* * * * *

The title of this project reminds us that the Voice of the One True God comes to us through the collective voices of many people who experienced God's special revelation. From the beginning God has been speaking, and He has chosen to speak through gifted and faithful people. The church has recognized in their voices a unique inspiration.

One problem with modern translations has been the tendency to homogenize the various voices so they all sound the same. Matthew sounds like Mark, Mark like Luke, Luke like John. Experts might be able to tell the difference, but the average reader is puzzled why there are four Gospels written in what seems to be the same voice. In fact, there are four Gospels written by four distinct writers, all bearing witness to the One True God who is reconciling the world through Jesus, but they do so to different audiences in different tones with different interests and concerns. In this translation we have made an effort to hear those voices and not homogenize them. As we read these sixty-six books and immerse ourselves in their stories, we recognize that the same God who inspired Abraham, Moses, David, and Amos meets us to call us to be reconciled and enter into a new life.

blog entry

January 3, 2012

The Bible in 4-D!

by David Capes

The first 3-D film I recall seeing was *Avatar* (2009). I sat down
in the theater with a big, icy Dr. Pepper at my right hand; a big,
steaming bag of popcorn at my left; and a big, clunky pair of 3-D
glasses wedged onto my forehead. When the movie began, I
slid the glasses over my eyes and for the next 171 minutes I was
caught up in an amazing bit of science fiction driven by stunning
visuals. I watched as bugs and bits of debris seemed to hang in
the air between me and the screen. I flinched more than once as
objects appeared to fly in my direction.

Somewhere in the middle of the movie, I slid the 3-D glasses
up and looked at the screen with my naked eyes. What I saw
was a series of hazy images layered over top of each other,
rimmed in blue and red. I realized, "I have no clue how this
works." But that didn't bother me. I just slid the glasses back
down over my eyes and everything became crystal clear again.

The New Testament gives us the gospel in 4-D. Four distinct
Gospels—Matthew, Mark, Luke and John—tell essentially the
same story but they do so in ways that are quite unique. From
the outside it may appear a bit hazy, but with the right tools
everything comes into focus.

Other Bible translations seem to flatten out the Gospels.
Mark reads like Luke, Matthew like John, and the distinct voices
of the different evangelists—the Gospel writers—are lost in
translation. Experts in the New Testament can guide readers
to the particular themes of each Gospel, but without a guide

people are left with a rather flat story that seems fuzzy around the edges.

With *The Voice New Testament* we have tried to recapture the authentic voices of the original authors. We did that by making a series of strategic decisions. Let me give you two examples. Since Matthew is the most Jewish Gospel, it made perfect sense to assign a large part of the work to a person with a Jewish background. Since Luke represents the most universal and sophisticated Gospel, it seemed right to assign much of the effort to a well-educated, articulate pastor and church leader. As a result, *The Voice New Testament* contains Gospels that don't sound and read the same. In other words, we get a better picture—a 4-D image of Jesus.

About 1800 years ago a Christian named Tatian tried to make one Gospel from the four. It was called the *Diatessaron*—literally, "through the four [Gospels]." It never caught on. For many reasons the Church preferred the four traditional Gospels to Tatian's single story. Today, I think the same dynamics are in play. The Jesus who lived then and lives today is no one-dimensional character. The four Gospels in *The Voice New Testament* provide us with four rich portraits of the most interesting and important person who ever lived.[3]

chapter
4

The Translation Philosophy

Whenever people render a text written in one language by another, they are engaged in translation. Still there are levels of formality or strictness in any translation process. Generally these levels fall on a scale between formal and functional (or dynamic) equivalence. But these approaches are not followed strictly by any Bible translation team, and most translations must mix formal with functional elements if they wish to communicate clearly to their target audiences. Realistically, languages are just too complex to be rendered successfully using a single approach. A strictly formal translation process will result in a text that is unreadable, obscuring rather than revealing the meaning of the Scripture to the intended audience. A strictly functional approach will result in a text that might communicate to a reader well what the original text means but not what it says.

The Voice translation team acknowledges the immense challenges involved in translation and offers what could be described as a mediating position on the formal-functional scale. We describe our approach as *contextual equivalence*. Recognizing that context is the most important factor in determining the meaning of a word, sentence, paragraph, or story, we have sought to create a Bible translation that preserves the relevant linguistic and literary features of the original text. A contextual equivalent translation technique takes seriously the cultural context of the original writers and audiences and then seeks to reproduce the meaning of those texts for our contemporary audience. It seeks to convey the original languages accurately while rendering the literary structure and character of a text in natural, readable, and meaningful English. This particular translation approach keeps in mind the smaller parts and the larger whole. In endeavoring to translate Sacred Scripture, The Voice captures uniquely the poetic imagery and literary artistry of the original in a way that is beautiful and meaningful.

For example, it is widely recognized that passages like Psalm 25 and Lamentations 3 in Hebrew are written in acrostic form. The Voice translation gives a nod to that classic literary expression by rendering these chapters in an English acrostic form as well. This, of course, is challenging because the Hebrew alphabet consists of twenty-two letters while English has twenty-six letters. Nevertheless the scholars and writers on The Voice team have endeavored to signal that behind these passages is a literary form that is unique, creative, and beautiful. Consider Lamentations 3:1–15:

> Afflicted, I have seen *and know* what it's like
>> to feel the rod of God's anger:
> An absence of light and only darkness.
>> *Darkness*—that's where God has driven me.
> Against me *and me alone,* over and over,
>> God raises His hand incessantly.
> Bones are broken, skin rubbed off, and my flesh wasted;
>> this is God's doing:
> Beseiged in hardship,
>> wrapped in *a husk of bitter poison and* trouble;
> Brought to darkness like those dead and decaying,
>> and left there alone to live.
> Cut off from every avenue of escape, God has fenced me in
>> and tied me up with heavy chains.
> Crying and carrying on do me no good;
>> God shuts out my prayer.

Closed in and blocked by walls of cut stone, what paths I have
    left,
    He has twisted and confused *my steps.*
Dangerous as a stalking lion or a lurking bear,
    God lies in wait for me.
Dragging me off the path and tearing me up,
    He has left me desolate.
Drawing back His bow, God aims
    straight at me with His own arrow.
Ever true arrows, ready in His quiver,
    now sink into my gut.
Echoing taunts ring 'round me from *the mouths of* my own
    people,
    laughing and joking about me all day long.
Enough! He has filled me with bitterness,
    saturated me with gall.

Attempting to reproduce the acrostic form is just one way the
translation team signaled its interest in exposing readers to the rich
literary forms in the Scriptures. In the next chapter we will give more
examples of how a contextual equivalence approach deals with bridging the gap between ancient and modern cultural horizons.

The Categories Don't Fit

The terms *dynamic equivalence* and *functional equivalence* were
coined by Dr. Eugene Nida, who was a leading scholar in the study of
linguistics and Bible translation. He used the phrase to describe an
approach to translation that attempts to reproduce the meaning of
the original text in one language (the source or donor language) in
the best possible target or receptor language (in our case, English).
In order to communicate effectively to a target audience, all translations have to make use of dynamic equivalence at some point in the
translation of any text.

Two other related descriptors are used to situate a Bible translation in the field. Some translations are judged to be "word-for-word" in contrast to those that are "thought-for-thought." Word-for-word translations generally claim to be more literal and therefore superior to those that are thought-for-thought. The critique is sometimes made that thought-for-thought translations reflect the interpretive opinions of the translators and are influenced by the contemporary culture more than word-for-word translations. There are four primary objections to these claims.

Translation Is Interpretation

Anyone who has studied translation theory or engaged in translation recognizes that it is impossible for translators to objectively render a text. The Italian expression says it bluntly: *Tradutorre, traditore* (the translator is a traitor). Even if it were possible and deemed useful to design a computer program that could mechanically translate the Scriptures into English, human subjectivity and judgment—in short, interpretation— would still come into play in various ways; for example, choosing which texts to translate, deciding which English word or words to use to translate a specific Hebrew, Greek, or Aramaic word, and determining how to apply specific grammatical and syntactical rules. Subjectivity and interpretive judgments are impossible to avoid in any translation and do not necessarily have a negative impact on a translation.

Words Are Thoughts

A strict distinction between *word* and *thought* must be questioned. After all, a word is merely an expressed thought. This fact becomes clear when dealing with people who are fluent in multiple languages. When they have a thought to express, they must choose which language to speak, then which word or words to use, and then which word order. We have all tried to find the right word or words to express what we are thinking. While there may be a line of distinction between a thought and a word, it is not a hard-and-fast line; it is at best a dotted line.

Meaning Has Context

Words generally do not have a single meaning; they have a range of meanings—what linguists refer to as a *semantic field*. Alister McGrath suggests that one factor that contributed to the elegance of the King James Bible was the translators' refusal to adopt a merely mechanical approach in translating from the Greek, Hebrew, and Aramaic. The Oxford and Cambridge scholars felt they were free to explore the semantic range of English words and phrases in order to render these sacred texts.[1] Their translation principle is set out clearly in the preface to the 1611 edition: "We have not tied ourselves to an uniformity of phrasing or an identity of words, as some peradventure would wish that we have done. . . . But that we should express the same notion in the same particular word, as for example, if we translate the Hebrew or Greek word once by 'purpose,' never to call it 'intent' . . . we thought to savour more of curiosity than wisdom."

Let's consider, for example, the translation of the Greek noun *dikaiosunē*. In one place the word might best be translated "justice," in another, "righteousness," in yet another, "equity" or "integrity," in still another, "that which is true or right." A translator must recognize that the context in which a word is used determines its meaning in another language.

In order to illustrate this, it may be helpful to start with the language we know best. Consider the meaning of the English word *stage*. It has a broad semantic field. To an actor the word *stage* refers to the raised platform on which she performs. To an engineer *stage* has to do with a particular section of a rocket engine as it separates after liftoff. A laboratory technician will carefully set an object he wants to examine on the *stage* of a microscope. To a psychologist *stage* refers to a particular portion of a person's life as in "the adolescent stage of human development." To a sociologist *stage* has to do with any major phase in the development of human societies, such as the hunter-gatherer stage. Angry workers might *stage* a strike while doctors puzzle over what *stage* a disease might be in. In the old west a mayor might wait for some dignitary to arrive on the afternoon *stage*. The point should be clear enough that words do not have a literal meaning; they may have a variety of meanings that will depend on context.

So one must understand the context in which a word is used in order to render carefully its meaning in another language. This context is not just semantic; it is also historical and social as we saw with the stage example above. Now consider The Voice translation of the title *Christos* as "the Anointed" or "Anointed One." We will have more to say about this translation later, but for now let's just consider the root meaning of the Greek word. Since the word means "to anoint (with oil)," translating *Christos* as "the Anointed" is faithful to the original language. But does that say enough? It speaks correctly to the meaning of the root word but not to the purpose for which one was anointed. This is why in select places we expanded the translation through what Darrell Bock has called *explanatory paraphrase*. The expanded translation "Jesus the Anointed, *the Liberating King*" captures something of the social and historical reality behind the confession. The earliest followers of Jesus came to see Him as God's agent, descended from King David, who was chosen ("anointed") to liberate the world from sin, death, corruption, and oppression.

To press this point even further, we need to recognize that words don't just *mean* things; they *do* things. Words have both meaning and function; they function within phrases, clauses, sentences, paragraphs, and stories in ways that are different from the definitions a person might find in a dictionary. When Matthew began his Gospel by naming Jesus Immanuel, which means "God with us" (Matthew 1:23), and ended it with Jesus' promise to be "with" His followers to the end of the age (Matthew 28:20), he was intentionally framing his story of Jesus to remind his audience of Jesus' true identity. He is "God with us." In this case the preposition "with" has meaning beyond its immediate use in a sentence; it has a purpose in the overall story of the Gospel.

Beyond this, however, we need to be aware of how words elicit emotions, memories, actions, and responses from those who hear (or read) them. When Matthew reminds his first readers that Jesus is descended from David who fathered Solomon through the wife of Uriah (Matthew 1:6), he is intentionally invoking one of the most embarrassing and humiliating moments in the history of Israel's celebrated king. This was a detail Matthew could have conveniently left out; instead he highlighted it in order to emphasize a significant aspect of Jesus' own story. Those who know the Old Testament story will sense the irony later in the Gospel when Jesus is called "a friend of sinners." In order to translate a text well, a person must consider not only what words mean but what they do and the memories and emotions (both good and bad) they evoke.

One Word May Not Be Enough

A word-for-word correspondence is difficult to maintain because translators may need multiple words in one language to express the meaning of a single word in another. Take for instance the Greek word *sōthēsetai* (Romans 10:13). Because of the way the English language works, it takes no fewer than four words to translate this single Greek verb: "he/she will be saved." Again, only the context can reveal who is going to be saved, what salvation entails, and when in the future it is to be realized.

When these four factors are considered, The Voice represents a hybrid of the formal and functional approaches. In some places The Voice follows what some may call a word-for-word translation; in others it expresses meaning in a thought-for-thought approach. But, as we have seen, there is no strict dichotomy between words and thoughts. This is necessitated contextually both by the original languages and by our target language (English). Responsibility to render the biblical languages carefully and to create a readable translation for an audience is not an either-or pursuit; a contextual equivalence translation seeks to be faithful and realistic to both tasks.

Avoiding Transliteration

When scholars began to translate the Old and New Testaments into the English language, they faced enormous challenges. Not only were powerful people opposed to rendering the sublime texts of Scriptures in a common language such as English, but the English language itself did not have all the words needed to reproduce meaningfully what the original languages were saying. The solution was to invent words that did not exist in English. One example is the word *Passover*.

In the fourteenth century when Wycliffe translated the New Testament into English, the word "Passover" did not exist in the English language. So when he came to those New Testament passages that referred to the Jewish Passover, Wycliffe transliterated the Latin word *pascha*—which is itself a transliteration of the Greek word *pascha*—into English as "pask" or "paske." As you see, transliteration involves representing the characters of one alphabet in another alphabet; it has nothing to do with translating the meaning of the word, only the sound of it. How readers and hearers may have reacted to this new word we do not know. Did they understand what it meant, or was some further explanation needed?

In 1535 when Tyndale translated the Old Testament into English, he decided to invent a new word in English to communicate the meaning behind the Hebrew root *pesach*:

> When your children ask you, "What does this ritual mean to you?" you will answer them, "It is the Passover sacrifice to the Eternal, for He passed over the houses of the Israelites *when we were slaves* in Egypt. And although He struck the Egyptians, He spared *our lives and* our houses." (Exodus 12:26–27)

The Hebrew root of the name of the Jewish festival alludes to the fact that God "passed over" the houses of the Israelites on His way to judging the cruelty of the Egyptian slave owners. Tyndale combined the two English words—"pass" with "over"—to create a single, new

57

word that carefully and accurately reproduced the meaning of the Hebrew word. Transliteration, at its best, can only reproduce the sounds made in another language, not their meaning. What Tyndale did by creating the word "Passover," The Voice translation has done for other key words that, until now, have not been accessible to a modern audience.

Christ

In its original Greek language, the New Testament refers to Jesus hundreds of times as *Christos*. Most English translations of Scripture render this *Christ*, which is not a translation but a transliteration. The unfortunate effect of this decision is that most readers today mistake *Christ* as a kind of second name for Jesus; that *Jesus* is His first name and *Christ* is His last name. In fact, *Christos* is not a name at all; it is a title. It is a Greek translation of the Hebrew title *Messiah*. So when the New Testament writers call Jesus "(the) Christ," they are making a bold claim—one of the central claims of the Christian faith—that "Jesus is the Messiah." While there was no single expectation about the Messiah in Jesus' day, many of His contemporaries would have recognized the Messiah as God's chosen, anointed agent whose task is to restore God's people and repair our broken world.

Because no single English word or phrase captures the richness of the term *Messiah* or *Christos*, we made a strategic decision in The Voice to translate *Christos* and not simply transliterate it. The root idea of *Christos* is derived from a Greek verb meaning "to anoint (with oil)." The act of anointing someone with oil was a way of setting that person apart for God's purpose. When people were anointed—kings and priests, for example—oil was poured over their heads, signifying that God had chosen them and that God's Spirit was coming upon them to empower them for the duties ahead. This is why we have decided to translate the title *Christ* as "the Anointed," "the Anointed One," or "God's Anointed," depending on context and narrative flow.

But there is another aspect of *Christos* we need to highlight. According to tradition, the Messiah is to be a Son of David, and as such He has a royal function to continue David's dynasty (1 Samuel 7:12–16) and to reign over a newly constituted kingdom. In order to become king, a person must have God's anointing. So from time to time, as we translated *Christos* "the Anointed," we have added the explanatory paraphrase "*the Liberating King*" to indicate to the reader the primary reason God elects and empowers Jesus in the first place. Jesus comes as the King of a new kind of a kingdom and exercises His royal power to rescue and liberate His creation. This liberation takes place on various levels, all of which are related.

One of the key passages to describe this reality is Luke 4:16–30. Not long after Jesus begins His public ministry, He returns to the synagogue in Nazareth—the town where He grew up—and reads the Scripture portion that day from Isaiah 61.

> The Spirit of the Lord the Eternal One is on Me.
> Why? Because the Eternal designated Me
>> to be His representative to the poor, to preach good news
>> to them.
> He sent Me to tell those who are held captive that they can now
> be set free,
>> and to tell the blind that they can now see.
> He sent me to liberate those held down by oppression.
> *In short, the Spirit is upon Me* to proclaim that now is the time;
>> this is the jubilee season of the Eternal One's grace.
>> (Luke 4:18–19)

From the way Jesus responds to the reading that day, it is clear that He understands His Spirit-enabled work to be about proclaiming the good news, releasing exiles and other political prisoners, healing the sick, and freeing the oppressed—in a word, *liberating* the poor, the captive, the sick, and the marginalized from whatever threatens them. But there is more.

The Scriptures declare that Jesus comes to liberate those made in God's image from the power and penalty of sin, which is the reason

God's good creation is so fouled up and disordered in the first place. In fact Paul tells the believers in Rome that all creation has been damaged by sin and longs for the day when God's true children are revealed and set free from the power of sin and death. When that day comes, Paul writes, creation itself will be liberated from its own slavery to corruption (Romans 8:18–25). By translating the phrase *Jesus Christos* as "Jesus the Anointed, *the Liberating King*" in key scriptural passages, we are reminded of the fuller meaning and an important truth: Jesus' kingdom and His liberating work extend beyond our hearts, beyond our politics, beyond our world.

It is important to note that early Christians referred to Jesus by a number of honorific titles in the Greek New Testament. They called Him *sōtēr* ("Savior"), *huios theou* ("Son of God"), *kyrios* ("Lord"), and other titles. For reasons that remain unclear, the title *Christos* was the only title not translated into the new language of the Western church. In the Latin translation *Christos* was rendered *Christus*, and in the English Bible tradition it became *Christ*. Interestingly, when the Christian faith moved north and east from its Jerusalem home, translators did not transliterate the Greek title *Christos*; they translated it *Meshikha*. This indicates that those scribes and scholars did not regard *Christos* as a name; they clearly understood the significance of the title and wanted to communicate that clearly to their audience.

Apostle

The Greek word *apostolos* is transliterated in most English Bible translations as *apostle*. The root of the Greek word means a person who acts as an agent of another by carrying out a special mission.[2] It refers chiefly to the original twelve called by Jesus (Matthew 10:2; Acts 1:26; Revelation 12:14), but by extension it came to refer to other specially gifted and prominent leaders (Acts 14:14; Romans 1:1). While seasoned Bible readers may have studied and come to understand the significance of this word, many new or first-time Bible readers will likely have little to go on to appreciate the importance of this office in the early church.

Rather than simply transliterating *apostolos* as "apostle," The Voice translation team decided to use an English word that might express better the meaning of the Greek word. While we considered other options such as *delegate* and *envoy*, we decided to translate every occurrence of *apostolos* as "emissary." The word emissary faithfully communicates the meaning of the Greek word and suggests the apostle has been specially chosen and designated to act as the agent of another. Furthermore, at the center of the word are the letters *m-i-s-s*, which recalls the important mission they are on for the risen Lord. There appears to be an important distinction between emissaries of the Lord Jesus and emissaries of the churches. The phrase "the emissaries of the Lord" refers to individuals to whom the risen Jesus appeared and gave a special charge (Matthew 28:19–20; Acts 9; Galatians 1). The emissaries of the churches were leaders chosen to represent the churches on particular missions.

Baptism

The Greek noun *baptisma* is transliterated in most English Bible translations as *baptism*. Likewise the Greek verb cognate with it, *baptizein*, is rendered *baptize*. As is clear, these English renderings are not translations but transliterations of the Greek word into a Latin or English alphabet. The meaning of the word, however, is evident. It refers to dipping something (or someone) in water for the express purpose of purifying or washing it. The historical antecedents for baptism—both John's baptism and Christian baptism—likely involve the ritual immersions that took place in specially designed pools known in Hebrew as *mikvaot*. For centuries archaeologists have been unearthing these pools all over Israel, particularly near sites of religious significance. Their prevalence indicates it was a common practice. Jewish purification rituals employing water provide the most relevant background to understanding the development and practice of Christian baptism.

The Voice translation team recognized the difficulty in translating a word such as baptism, particularly since Christian traditions practice baptism in many different ways. Some communities baptize infants; others baptize only believers. Some churches baptize by total immersion in water; others by sprinkling or pouring water on the head. Since the word could likely be misunderstood by those outside the Christian tradition, we decided to employ transliteration along with an explanatory phrase. The explanatory phrase used generally offers a reason for which a person is immersed in the water, namely, to wash or clean him or her from impurity. Furthermore, Christian baptism adds another layer of meaning since it is practiced as a rite of initiation into the Christian faith. In other words, through baptism a person participates in the death, burial, and resurrection of Jesus (Romans 6:3–6).

For now, let us consider these two examples: when John the Baptist is introduced in Mark 1:4, he is described as "preaching that people should be ritually cleansed through baptism *with water as a sign of* both their changed hearts and God's forgiveness of their sins." When Paul discusses the significance of baptism, he writes, "Did someone forget to tell you that when you were initiated into Jesus the Anointed through baptism's ceremonial washing, we entered into His death?" (Romans 6:3). Although the Greek root *baptisma* refers primarily to the act of dipping something in water, the purpose for the dipping is clearly in view for both John's and Christian baptism. In both cases a person is dipped in water to cleanse or wash away impurity. In John's case baptism signifies repentance, a changed heart, and the assurance of God's forgiveness. In Christian baptism a believer is washed as a prelude to beginning a new life by participating in the death, burial, and resurrection of Jesus.

Angels

The Greek word *aggelos* (pronounced än'-ge-los) is transliterated in English Bibles as *angel*. The Greek word itself means "messenger" or "envoy" of another. The angels have a variety of functions in the Christian Scriptures. In the Old Testament, for example, the angels (*mal'akim* in Hebrew) go by a variety of names such as *spirits, sons of*

God, and *watchers*. They sit on the divine council (1 Kings 22:19–23; Job 1—2) and exercise the will of God on earth. Some angels preside over the nations (Deuteronomy 32:8–9) while the principal angel, Michael, exercises God's reign over His covenant people Israel (Daniel 10:13).

In the New Testament it is clear that the *angelos* is a supernatural or heavenly being who acts as the messenger of God (Matthew 1:20). In some cases the creature is understood as a guardian of some sort (Acts 12:15). In still others the *angeloi* (plural) serve as mediators between God and humanity (Galatians 3:19). Like the Holy Spirit, angels provide guidance and direction to early Christian leaders in key moments as they are on mission (Acts 8:26–39; 27:23). It is often the case that people who have encounters with angels are struck with fear, perhaps because of their glorious appearance (Daniel 8:15–27; Luke 1:8–20, 26–38, 2:8–19). All biblical angels are described in masculine terms. The only named angels in the Scriptures are Michael and Gabriel. In other Jewish texts from the period, other named angels include Raphael, Uriel, and Yahoel. All these are masculine names. These remarks provide some context for understanding the nature and role of the angels in Scripture.

The problem for translators involves not so much the ancient context, which is relatively clear, but the modern one. Most people today envision angels as rather banal creatures. They look much like humans and exist primarily to help wayward souls realize their full potential. Consider the classic American film *It's a Wonderful Life* (1946) in which the angel, Clarence, arrives to help George Bailey (played by Jimmy Stewart) who is about to commit suicide. Clarence intervenes, saves George, and subsequently earns his wings. In 1994 CBS premiered a popular American drama called *Touched by an Angel*. The series ran until 2003. The angels (played by Roma Downey and Della Reese) are assigned to provide guidance and messages from God to various people who find themselves at particularly difficult crossroads in life. If you search for images of angels on the Internet, you will discover page after page of feminine, winged creatures or chubby cherubs. Under the influence of pop culture, angels have little in common with the masculine, awesome, fearsome, and powerful creatures depicted in the Scriptures. In the Bible the *angeloi* exist at the boundary of this world and heavenly realms announcing and exercising God's will, not helping people realize theirs.

As with other key words, The Voice translation team thought the disconnect between the ancient and modern contexts make it imprecise to transliterate the Greek word *angelos* as *angel*; instead we decided to translate the word by its meaning, that is, "heavenly messenger." This phrase faithfully reproduces the meaning of the Hebrew *mal'ak* and Greek *aggelos* ("messenger"). The addition of "heavenly" to the phrase indicates that these beings come to earth from heaven in order to represent heaven's interests here.

Names

The decision to avoid transliterations in The Voice did not extend to the names of people and places. Although names often have meaning in the Scripture, The Voice followed the spelling conventions for names that have recently become standard. A survey of all English translations demonstrates the variety of ways names have been spelled. The Hebrew name *Yesha'yahu*, for example, was spelled *Isaias* in some earlier versions; The Voice follows the conventional spelling, *Isaiah*. Similarly, the Hebrew name of Isaac's wife, *Rivkah*, is often spelled *Rebecca* in English translations; we opted instead for the more Hebraic spelling *Rebekah*. The Hebrew name of Daniel's colleague in exile, *Aved-N'go*, is often spelled *Abednego*; The Voice translation chose to hyphenate the name *Abed-nego* in keeping with the more Hebraic sound. But the Scriptures contain more than Hebrew names. The exile forced the Hebrews to live for a time alongside the Babylonians and Persians who left an indelible mark on God's people and their language.

In the book of Esther, for example, the Persian king goes by the name *Achasverosh*. Recent versions have transliterated this *Ahasuerus*, while some have referred to him by his more popular Greek name, *Xerxes*. The Voice team used the transliteration that has recently become standard: *Ahasuerus*. The citadel of Ahasuerus was a city known as *Shushan*. Some versions transliterated the word exactly while others rendered it *Susan*. The Voice referred to his palace city as *Susa* in keeping with recent trends.

The Voice translation employs transliterations of the names of all people and places with the exception of the divine name, *YHWH*, often referred to as *the tetragrammaton*. As we discuss in chapter 6, out of respect for the divine name and in appreciation for how the Jewish and Christian traditions regard the divine name, the team opted to translate the name "The Eternal."

chapter
5

Contextual Equivalence in Practice

In the front matter of The Voice Bible, the translation approach is described *contextual equivalence*. At the heart of this approach is the commitment to take seriously both the context of the original writers and audiences—as much as they can be known—and the modern context of our readers. Our intended audience occupies a very different time, culture, and language from those who first wrote, edited, or heard these sixty-six books.

What a word or expression means today is often at odds with what it meant thousands of years ago. While it would be impossible to show how a contextually equivalent approach influenced the entire project, we can demonstrate in a few key passages the kind of thought that went into this project. Let us begin "in the beginning" with the book of Genesis.

In the Beginning—Genesis 1

The book of Genesis begins in memorable fashion. The King James Version offers a straightforward translation of its opening verse:

> In the beginning God created the heavens and the earth.

This is a brilliant, simple, and accurate translation of the Hebrew. Modern translations have followed it nearly verbatim. But as we thought about our target audience, it dawned on several of us how different the word "heavens" and "earth" are today compared to the ancients. When the writer of Genesis said, "God created the heavens and the earth," he was expressing a particular cosmology. *Cosmology* is a technical term for how people think and talk about the world around them. The cosmology in Genesis represents a fairly simple and straightforward way of understanding the world.

The Hebrew word translated "the heavens" in Genesis 1:1 means everything above your head. Well, what is above your head? The sky. The clouds. In this sense the Scriptures can say that the birds fly in the heavens. The sun, moon, and stars. And water, lots of water. How do we know? Water falls from the sky in the form of rain, sleet, and snow. There is a lot of water up there.

What about "the earth"? For the ancients "the earth" meant everything below your feet. Well, what is below your feet? Soil, grass, clay, sand, rock, and—if you dig down a bit—water, lots of water. Water above and water below. That is why water figures so prominently in the Genesis account.

So the combination of "the heavens and the earth" means "everything." Nothing is left out. Now in Hebrew there is no word that corresponds to our concept of the universe, but in a sense that is what Genesis is saying. That's why The Voice translation of Genesis 1:1 reads:

> In the beginning, God created *everything:* the heavens *above* and the earth *below. Here's what happened:*

Today the words *heaven* and *heavens* are used in a variety of ways the writer of Genesis never intended. As we discussed earlier, the semantic field (that is, the range of meanings) of the word is broad. Let's consider a few examples. People talk about the heavens as the place above where the stars burn brightly; it is another word—perhaps with more romantic or poetic overtones—for *space.* But it is also common for believers to say that when people die they go to heaven. Does that mean that disembodied spirits are floating out there among the stars in space? This has given rise to the silly notion that when people die their souls sit on the clouds strumming harps somewhere up there. But Christians also pray, "Our Father in heaven." Does that mean that somewhere out there in space God really dwells? With such a broad range of meanings, it is easy to see how people might be confused.

Genesis is simpler and more elegant than that. In Genesis God creates everything you see above. Genesis is not discussing the origins of God or God's abode; it assumes God's existence. It is also not talking the creation of the place where the faithful go after death. What the first book of the Bible does affirm is that if you look up, everything you see God has created.

How about the word *earth*? Today when modern people think about earth, they think of it as the third planet from the sun, the "blue planet," Carl Sagan's "pale blue dot" among the family of planets.[1] With a modicum of scientific knowledge, we can imagine the earth's orb rushing around the sun at over sixty thousand miles per hour in its annual orbit as seasons come and go. The earth as planet is very different than the simple and elegant cosmology in Genesis describing everything you see below your feet.

The modern uses of the words *heaven* and *earth* today are not better than the way ancients used them; they are just different. As a translation interested in both the ancient and modern contexts, we have to think about these issues as we are taking ancient texts into our modern world. If we want to communicate carefully what the ancients had to say, we need to think about the words as they would have understood them.

Finally, we added the explanatory phrase "*Here's what happened*" to correct a fundamental misunderstanding people often have of the Genesis creation story. The wrong way to read Genesis 1:1 is that God created the heavens and earth, and then understand the following verses as what happens next, after God created them. The writer of Genesis would have us see it otherwise. These verses back up and tell us what happens *on the way to* God creating, ordering, and then filling creation with creatures.

Life Is Fleeting—Ecclesiastes 1

Ecclesiastes is considered by many one of the most radical books in the Bible. Scholars classify it as an example of Jewish wisdom literature because it reflects on life, its frustrations, and its meaning. Wisdom, in the Hebrew tradition, is all about living life well and making good decisions. Some people love Ecclesiastes and count it as one of their favorites; others ignore it almost completely because they find it so negative and dismissive in tone.

The philosophizing begins immediately with words and expressions that are taken as thematic throughout the book. The King James translators rendered it, "Vanity of vanities, saith the Preacher, vanity of vanities, all is vanity" (Ecclesiastes 1:2). Many modern translations have followed the King James Version in translating this verse. The important Hebrew word here translated "vanity" is *hebel*. The word *hebel* means "vapor" or "breath." It serves as a metaphor or sign of what is temporary or fleeting, but the expression is difficult to convey in English. One early indication of how it was read by pious Jews is found in the Greek translation of the Hebrew Bible called the Septuagint. The translators used the Greek word *mataiotēs* to translate the Hebrew *hebel*; it is widely accepted that this Greek word means *futility*. The Greek translation provides some guidance to how Greek-speaking Jews would have understood the expression in the centuries before the birth of Jesus. If we were to render the text literally, we would end up with something like this:

"Breath of breaths," says the Teacher, "Breath of breaths, all is breath."

The question, of course, for any translator is, what does the phrase "breath of breaths" mean? How do we render that in smooth, natural English? Consider the choices made by other translations:

> "Meaningless! Meaningless!"
> says the Teacher.
> "Utterly meaningless!
> Everything is meaningless." (NIV)

> "Everything is meaningless," says the Teacher, "completely
> meaningless!" (NLT)

> "Futile! Futile!" laments the Teacher,
> "Absolutely futile! Everything is futile!" (NEB)

Recently a number of scholars have suggested that the phrase *hebel hebalim* should be translated as "absurdity of absurdities."[2] That, along with the versions above, each represent a good-faith effort to get at the meaning of a difficult Hebrew expression.

To a large degree, the problem for a translator has to do not with what words and expressions meant then, but what they mean now. Let's consider the translation found in the KJV and all those versions that follow it. What do postmoderns think when they hear the word *vanity*? Well, not to be flippant, but for most in the reading audience a vanity refers to the cabinet in the bathroom where teeth are brushed, faces are washed, and personal hygiene items are stored. Obviously that is not what the text is talking about. Maybe they think of vanity as an inflated sense of a person's self-worth. In that sense "vanity of vanities" would be understood as a lament over the dominance and ubiquity of pride in human experience. While pride and arrogance are dangerous vices, they are not the concern of the teacher in Ecclesiastes 1:2. Perhaps it would be better to translate *hebel* by the expression *in vain* rather than simply *vanity*.

Now what about "meaningless," the translation of *hebel* found in the New International and New Living Translations? The problem of life's meaninglessness characterizes life in the modern world. While the existential movement is a modern and postmodern development, the existential crisis faced by all people since the dawn of humanity is clearly etched on the chapters of Ecclesiastes. What is not clear is whether Ecclesiastes is actually teaching that life is meaningless, that everything is meaningless. In fact, as you read through the book, the teacher finds meaning in life in numerous places. While we do not have time to rehearse all those now, the book ends famously with the advice of the teacher: "And, when all is said and done, here is the last word: worship in reverence the one True God, and keep His commands, for this is *what God expects* of every person. For God will judge every action—including everything done in secret—whether it be good or evil" (Ecclesiastes 12:13–14).

Such an ending makes it difficult to argue that the key verse of Ecclesiastes should be interpreted to mean that everything in life is meaningless in a modern, existential sense. Some things do have meaning, particularly worshiping the One True God and obeying His teachings. In the end God does expect certain things from His children, and He judges the actions performed by His creatures even if they are frustrated and confused by the ins and outs of life. So our lives and actions do have meaning.

Ecclesiastes was one of the last books we finished in the Old Testament. The scholars and writers who worked on it struggled to find the best way in English to express the meaning behind the key phrase *hebel hebalim*. Dr. Nancy deClaissé-Walford, one of the Hebrew scholars, offered an interesting word picture: *hebel hebalim* is like trying to catch hold of a breath. Her suggestion shaped how we viewed not only this verse but much of the rest of the book. Here is The Voice translation of Ecclesiastes 1:2:

> Life is fleeting, like a passing mist.
> *It is like trying to catch hold of a breath;*
> All vanishes like vapor; everything is a great vanity.

As you can see, this translation is complex. *Hebel hebalim* combines various images—a passing mist, a vanishing vapor, trying to

Contextual Equivalence in Practice

catch hold of breath. The point of these images is to underscore that life is fleeting, nothing is permanent, and everything in this world is provisional. In ways The Voice translation of Ecclesiastes 1:2, by stacking various images, reads like an amplified version.

When the word *hebel* appears again and again in the text—nearly thirty times in all—it is clearly meant to echo the initial teaching. In these cases the word *fleeting* is used and combined with other, similar images: "I have witnessed all that is done under the sun, and indeed, all is fleeting, like trying to embrace the wind. . . . As I continued musing over all I had accomplished and the hard work it took, *I concluded that* all this, too, was fleeting, like trying to embrace the wind. Is there any real gain *by all our hard work* under the sun?" (Ecclesiastes 1:14, 2:11). As these verses indicate, there is another, related phrase in Ecclesiastes that is repeated throughout the book (1:14, 17; 2:11; 4:4, 16; 6:9). It reinforces and expands the initial declaration, *hebel hebalim*, and has been translated in a number of ways:

- vexation of spirit (KJV)
- grasping for the wind (NKJV)
- striving after wind (NAS)
- chasing the wind (NET and NLT)
- chasing after the wind (NEB)

As we considered how to render this important image in Ecclesiastes, Dr. deClaissé-Walford brought to our attention that the Hebrew word translated "chasing" has another meaning in Hebrew, namely, "female companion." It implies that the object is something desired. So under her guidance, we translated most of the occurrences of that phrase "embracing the wind": "It is better to enjoy what our eyes see than to long for what our *roving* appetites desire. This, too, is fleeting, like trying to embrace the wind" (Ecclesiastes 6:9). In the end The Voice translation of Ecclesiastes challenges the conclusion that the book itself is overly negative. It also undermines any attempt to view life and human experience as meaningless, particularly in the modern existential sense. Dr. deClaissé-Walford's translation notes express it well:

> All that to say that my take on Eccelesiastes is not at all negative. It is a commentary on life, a musing on life that says this life has been given to us by God; it is a mystery, and most of it we simply cannot understand. And the advice of the teacher says we should—enjoy and celebrate the life we have been given.

In a contextual equivalent approach, translators cannot be concerned simply with what words, expressions, and idioms meant in their ancient contexts; they must also keep in mind what words mean today. Words such as vanity, meaningless, and absurdity come with connotative baggage that may miss the heart of what a word like *hebel* means. Since *hebel* is a metaphor meaning "breath" or "vapor," an English metaphorical expression "like trying to catch hold of a breath" stirs the readers' imagination to catch hold of what the Teacher is trying to say.

Jesus' Family Tree—Matthew 1

The New Testament begins with a genealogy of Jesus. Many modern readers find the list of names irrelevant, so they often skip over Matthew 1 to get to the "good stuff." Few people take the time to read the chapter. Fewer still bother to study it in depth. For those who do, there is a great deal of insight waiting for them into who Jesus is and what He came to do.

You may hear Matthew 1 referred to as the "begat chapter" because of the way the Greek verb *egennēsen* was translated in the King James Version:

> Abraham begat Isaac; and Isaac begat Jacob; and Jacob begat Judas and his brethren; and Judas begat Phares and Zara of Thamar; and Phares begat Esrom; and Esrom begat Aram. (Matthew 1:2–3 KJV)

The New King James Version made slight adjustments in punctuation and spelling of names, but kept the "begot" language.

> Abraham begot Isaac, Isaac begot Jacob, and Jacob begot Judah and his brothers. Judah begot Perez and Zerah by Tamar, Perez begot Hezron, and Hezron begot Ram.

The New International Version updated the language for a modern audience by translating the Greek *egennēsen* with the phrase "was the father of":

> Abraham was the father of Isaac, Isaac the father of Jacob, Jacob the father of Judah and his brothers, Judah the father of Perez and Zerah, whose mother was Tamar, Perez the father of Hezron, Hezron the father of Ram.

The Voice translation also uses the phrase "was the father of" to render the Greek verb:

> Abraham was the father of Isaac; Isaac was the father of Jacob; Jacob was the father of Judah and of Judah's 11 brothers; Judah was the father of Perez and Zerah (and Perez and Zerah's mother was Tamar); Perez was the father of Hezron; Hezron was the father of Ram.

The Voice's unique translation of Matthew's genealogy is not found in how it translates the Greek verb; it is located in the helps it provides the modern reader to understand the context of the genealogy. These are placed in the text as supplied words or commentary surrounding the text. As we have said, a contextually equivalent translation takes seriously both the ancient context as well as the modern. So let's consider Matthew's audience and his context.

Matthew's Gospel is widely understood to be the most Jewish Gospel. He is writing as a Jewish follower of Jesus to other Jews, some of whom were themselves followers of Jesus. So instead of seeing the genealogy as a list of meaningless names—as moderns might be prone to do—Matthew's audience would have known these people as their physical and spiritual ancestors. Furthermore, if they were observant Jews who attended synagogue regularly, they would have heard stories about their ancestors read time and again as the Hebrew Scriptures were opened each week. Each name was therefore associated with a relative and a set of deeds, some noble and others not so much.

Recognizing this, The Voice translation attempts to fill out some of the stories associated with the names. For example, after Jesus is introduced as descended from Abraham, the commentary provides this bit of detail: "It [the family history of Jesus] begins with Abraham, whom God called into a special, chosen, covenanted relation, and who was the founding father of the nation of Israel." When Tamar is mentioned as the mother of Perez and Zerah, the embedded commentary alludes to part of her story: "Tamar was Judah's widowed daughter-in-law; she dressed up like a prostitute and seduced her father-in-law, all so she could keep this very family line alive." These brief comments do not tell the entire story, of course, but they are an index to the story behind the persons mentioned. Now this kind of information would have been obvious to Matthew's original Jewish audience, but it is largely lost on a twenty-first-century audience, especially first-time Bible readers.

All first-century AD Jews looked to Abraham as their father—physically and spiritually—and most of them would have known the shameful saga of how Judah unknowingly propositioned his daughter-in-law and impregnated her. Modern readers, however, have little or no context for seeing Jesus' family tree as any more than a list of disconnected names. The Voice translation selectively supplies some of that context. There are too many names and too many stories to tell. Most modern Bible editions will just provide cross-references in the margins in case a person wants to follow those references to know more about the historical context. The Voice translation, however, brings the story to the reader with the use of embedded commentary and supplied words in the translation.

But there is even more to Matthew's genealogy. Matthew structures his genealogy and includes certain people and references to foreshadow key aspects of Jesus' life, His character, and the Kingdom message He proclaims. First, Matthew's genealogy contains names and references to several women (Tamar, Rahab, Ruth, Bathsheba, and Mary). This is unusual because at the time women are not included in genealogies, despite their obvious function in "begetting" children. It was a man's world, pure and simple. The inclusion of women signals Matthew's original audience that women will play an increasingly important role in Jesus' career and the arrival of God's kingdom. Second, by highlighting certain people and their stories, Matthew's genealogy intentionally reminds the audience that Jesus' family history includes people with deeply broken and messed-up lives. Had Matthew wanted to sanitize Jesus' ancestors, he could have strategically left out those whose shameful acts brought disgrace upon Abraham's family. Instead, he emphasizes those moments in order to signal his audience that Jesus would be a friend of sinners and die on their behalf. To put it another way, if your great-grandfather was a well-known horse thief, you would not have to lead with that as you are telling your own story. Matthew, however, does not cover up the embarrassing episodes that make up Jesus' family; he brings them out front and puts them on display. Third, Matthew includes the names of well-known outsiders (non-Jews such as Rahab and Ruth) in Jesus' family history. Again, he could have skirted those details had they not suited him, but it did suit him to point out that Jesus came not just for the lost sheep of Israel but to welcome outsiders into the Kingdom. Finally, Matthew structures his genealogy into three lists of fourteen names. These numbers are significant in Jewish gematria, a kind of spiritual numerology. The number three is associated with completion, and the number fourteen is associated with the name of King David. At a time when some Jews were insisting that Jesus was not the Messiah, Matthew uses his genealogy to show that Jesus is the true Son of David (an important messianic title), and he finds it even in the numbers.

Since many in Matthew's original audience were Jews well acquainted with the ancestors and stories of Israel, they would have caught the theological significance of much of what is behind Jesus' family history. A modern audience, however, does not have the background to be able to see these narrative connections. This is why The Voice translation team decided to provide its readers with supplied words and embedded commentary in and around the text itself. Such helps allow the reader to have a fuller sense of who Jesus' ancestors were and why their stories are so compelling.

God Expressed His Love—John 3:16

John 3:16 may be the best-known and most memorized verse in the English Bible. Its uncomplicated, graceful message serves as an apt summary of John's Gospel. When comparing translations, most people turn to John 3:16 to see how close the new translation is to what is familiar. For humans familiarity means comfort. If a translation is close to what is familiar, they will likely view it favorably. If it steers too far from the cadence and verbiage they know, they will likely view it negatively.

Most Bible-reading Christians are well acquainted with the strains of the King James translation of John 3:16:

> For God so loved the world, that he gave his only begotten Son, that whosoever believeth in him should not perish, but have everlasting life.

By in large, modern English versions have followed the King James; any changes made simply update some of the language:

> For God so loved the world that He gave His only begotten Son, that whoever believes in Him should not perish but have everlasting life. (NKJV)

> For God so loved the world that he gave his one and only Son,
> that whoever believes in him shall not perish but have eternal
> life. (NIV)

> For God so loved the world, that he gave his only Son, that
> whoever believes in him should not perish but have eternal
> life. (ESV)

These translations faithfully reproduce the meaning of John 3:16 from the original Greek. The slight differences between them relate primarily to differences in the Greek texts being translated.

The Voice translation of John 3:16 departs from the King James Version and these other translations in strategic ways based upon how the intended audience might understand key words.

> For God expressed His love for the world in this way: He gave
> His only Son so that whoever believes in Him will not face
> everlasting destruction, but will have everlasting life.

There are three major ways in which The Voice translation differs from previous translations. Each represents a contextual difference between the ancient texts and twenty-first-century understanding.

First, modern readers will take the word *love* primarily as a feeling-oriented word. Love expresses what we like or what we are naturally attracted to. It expresses our feelings toward someone or something. In America people use the word *love* in expressions as broad as: "I love my children"; "I love my job"; "I love my iPhone"; "I love Starbucks coffee." Now what a parent means when she says, "I love my children," is quite different than when she says, "I love Starbucks coffee." So the word *love* both as a noun and a verb offers a challenge for the translator. From what we know of John's original context, *love* is action-oriented not feeling-oriented. John 3:16 is not conveying that God sent His only Son into the world because He had a warm, fuzzy feeling toward it. He may have—we don't know—but that does not seem to be John's concern in chapter 3. John is saying that God acts in the best interest of those He loves; this includes everyone who inhabits this disordered world. In order to move *love* from feeling- to action-oriented, we elected to translate the phrase this way: "For God expressed His love for the world. . . ."

A second difference has to do with the tiny word often translated "so": "For God so loved the world. . . ." In English the word *so* can mean a variety of things: (1) to a great degree or very much, (2) most certainly or indeed, or (3) in the same manner/way. I once heard a sermon in which the pastor took the word *so* in the sense of *very*, and he waxed on and on repeating phrases such as "so amazingly loved," "so wonderfully loved," "so fantastically loved." Now God's love may well be described as amazing, wonderful, and fantastic, but that does not seem to be John's point. The Greek word translated *so* in most versions is better understood as option three above: "God expressed His love for the world *in this way*. . . ." What follows, namely, "He gave His only Son . . ." demonstrates the depth of God's action-oriented love for the world. The translators of the New English Bible understood this:

> For this is the way God loved the world: He gave his one and
> only Son, so that everyone who believes in him will not perish
> but have eternal life.

The Voice could have translated the word this way: "For God expressed His love for the world *so*. . . ." But again "so" could be misunderstood. The phrase "in this way" is more clear and flows better in public reading.

A third difference concerns how modern readers interpret the word *perish*. For most virgin-readers of Scripture, *perish* means "to die or be destroyed," "to disappear," "to be ruined or spoiled." It is more common in British usage than American. Now John 3:16 does not teach that a person who believes in Jesus will not die physically; indeed Jesus-followers die and should expect to. In reality, a contextual reading of the entire Gospel sets before the reader two possibilities: (1) "everlasting destruction" and (2) "everlasting life." Both destinies assume that these distinct futures are the result of God's judgment and not just a natural consequence. This is why we translated the phrase "face everlasting destruction." The Voice translation picks up on the Jewish context of John's discourse and sets out clearly the two options or ways before them: the way of destruction and the way of life. These two eschatological realities are "everlasting."

While the terms *everlasting* and *eternal* could be synonyms, the word *everlasting* implies a coming age in which time never ends. It is based on the Jewish eschatological hope the rabbis called "the world to come" (*ha-olam ha-ba*). The phrase in the New Testament often translated "eternal/everlasting life" may be better understood as "life in the age to come." *Eternal*, on the other hand, for many people implies a state of timelessness. The Jewish hope in the age to come is not a timeless existence as we see implied in the Platonic tradition but an existence in which time never ends. This is why we opted for the phrase *everlasting life* rather than *eternal life*.

As you can tell, ancient and modern contexts shaped how The Voice translation team looked at John 3:16 and determined how we rendered this key verse. To understand this text properly, it is important to (1) move away from a feelings-oriented view of love, (2) understand the contextual meaning of the Greek word typically translated *so*, and (3) grasp that believing in Jesus forms the basis of whether individuals experience everlasting destruction or everlasting life.

God's Restorative Justice—Romans and 2 Corinthians

There is a phrase in Paul's letters that is notoriously difficult to translate: *dikaiosunē theou*.[3] It occurs at key moments in major letters like Romans and 2 Corinthians. Most often the phrase is translated into English as "the righteousness of God."

> For I am not ashamed of the gospel, for it is the power of God
> for salvation to everyone who believes, to the Jew first and also

to the Greek. For in it [the gospel] the righteousness of God is revealed from faith to faith; as it is written, "But the righteous man shall live by faith." (Romans 1:16–17 NASB)

But now apart from the Law the righteousness of God has been manifested, being witnessed by the Law and the Prophets, even the righteousness of God through faith in Jesus Christ for all those who believe; for there is no distinction. (Romans 3:21–22 NASB)

For a number of avid Bible readers, the New American Standard Bible is the preferred translation. Many ministers preach from it and have done so for years. It may well be the most literal translation into English available that is somewhat readable. If a person has the time, interest, and skill in doing a word study, it is a helpful translation to have around. Unfortunately for seasoned and unseasoned readers alike, the NASB often obscures the meaning of important passages. Furthermore the way the words sit on the page makes this version difficult to follow. People without a strong background in Scripture are often left scratching their heads after reading from this translation.

So what does the phrase *dikaiosunē theou* refer to? It is an important question. Without getting that straight you will not be able to make heads or tails out of what Paul is saying in these key passages. Scholars, by the way, have been debating the significance of this phrase in these letters for centuries. So it is no easy task.

While translating The Voice, the team spent a great deal of time working through Paul's language in these passages. They considered the context of Paul's world and gospel. They pondered how certain words such as *righteousness* are read, understood, and function within the modern context. Bridging the gap between ancient and modern is no easy chore. In the end, the team developed this faithful and helpful rendering of this evocative phrase:

For I am not *the least bit* embarrassed about the gospel. *I won't shy away from it,* because it is God's power to save every person who believes: first the Jew, and then the non-Jew. You see, in the good news, God's restorative justice is revealed. *And as we will see,* it begins with and ends in faith. As the Scripture declares: "By faith the just will obtain life." (Romans 1:16–17)

But now *for the good news:* God's restorative justice has entered the world, independent of the law. Both the law and the prophets told us this day would come. This redeeming justice comes through the faithfulness of Jesus, the Anointed, who makes salvation a reality for all who believe—without the slightest partiality. (Romans 3:21–22)

The translation team reckoned that this reading would help shed light on what Paul is getting at in these verses, for virgin as well as veteran readers. Still the editorial team decided to add some commentary to help people think through the emissary's argument.

The twin phrases *God's restorative justice* and *this redeeming justice* refer to the same reality and translate the same Greek phrase. The stacking of *redeeming* on to *restorative* offers a fuller sense to describe the effect of what the apostle thinks Jesus has accomplished on the cross. For Paul the good news—the gospel—is located in history in the incarnation and sacrificial death of Jesus. By "God's restorative justice" Paul means first that justice and rightness belong to God; they reflect His character. God, and no one else, determines what is right and what is just. But as we all know, character is reflected in action. *Justice* and *righteousness* are nouns of action. This means that God's justice must express itself in some way. So it is in the nature of a just God to act, to restore, to redeem, in short to repair what is wrong with the world. This, according to Paul, God did primarily through His Son, Jesus the Anointed, the Liberating King.

Paul would not shy away from these bold claims; for him the gospel is power. It is God's power to restore the world to what it can and ought to be. But how do we get in on what God is doing? Well, Paul says, it begins with and ends in faith. It begins with God's faithfulness to His creation, then His covenant people. It continues with Jesus' faithfulness to God to enter our broken realm to give Himself in love to begin its repair. It ends with us, hearing and responding in faith and following faithfully in His footsteps.

The term *justice* today is used broadly within public and legal discourse. People who have committed heinous acts are brought to justice when they appear before a court and the verdict is rendered against them. The United States Department of Justice is charged with the responsibility of enforcing the law and making sure justice is done domestically. The phrase *social justice* is used today to describe a number of movements toward a society where every person is treated with dignity, where basic human rights are affirmed and practiced, and where all people have the opportunity to better themselves. The sticking point, of course, has to do with all the political divides and agendas that make it difficult even to define justice much less what it looks like in society or how to realize it.

The phrase *God's restorative justice* as used in The Voice translation acknowledges God as the source of justice; it begins with and ends with Him. God defines what justice is and what a just society will be. Furthermore, God is the only one who can actualize justice and "make it so" in society. Human beings at our very best can only recognize that things are not as they should be. We can long for injustice to give way to justice but not make it happen on our own. Our best faith efforts will be hijacked by personal agendas and murky motives. Equipped with consciences, reason, and tradition, we can analyze and figure out provisional solutions to moderately sized problems, but we cannot finally and definitively deal with injustice. The Scriptures affirm that only God can deal finally with what is wrong with the world and set it right. God is the one who can repair what is broken, redeem what is lost, and restore what is disordered. For Paul the fix is already on.

The Philippian Hymn—Philippians 2:6–11

A contextually equivalent version must take into consideration not only the words but the forms in which words come to the reader. A case in point is the well-known hymn in Philippians 2:6–11, often referred to in Latin as the *Carmen Christi* or "Hymn to Christ." Now, to be clear, these verses do not contain a hymn addressed to the Anointed One but a hymn addressed to the world about Him. It is a testimony song, of sorts, that rehearses His preexistent status, descent in the incarnation, crucifixion, resurrection, and exaltation. Paul employs this hymn in his letter from prison to the believers in Philippi in order to encourage them to follow the Lordly example of Jesus in service and sacrifice to others.

For centuries scholars have taken note of these remarkable verses, and it is the conclusion of most that they represent an early Christian hymn that the imprisoned emissary incorporates into his letter. In other words Philippians 2:6–11 contains a preformed hymn that Paul adopts as part of his letter. He may, of course, have been the composer of these exalted lines; but from the form and style of them, it is unlikely he made them up as he went along. It would be as if you were writing a letter to a friend who needed encouragement and you wrote,

And don't forget, my friend:

> "Amazing grace, how sweet the sound,
>   that saved a wretch like me.
> I once was lost but now I'm found,
>   Was blind but now I see."[4]

If your friend knew the song "Amazing Grace," it would be easy to excerpt it and see it as poem. Perhaps if the early Christians Paul addressed knew this Christ hymn, they would have recognized it for what it was and been encouraged by his use of it.

Translating poetry and hymns from one language to another is challenging. The original rhythm and meter cannot be approximated without significant changes to the content of the song or poem. If there are other literary features such as assonance, alliteration, or rhyming, they cannot be duplicated easily in the target language. A number of modern translations do not even convey the hymn-like character of these verses to their readers. The NASB, for example, formats each verse as if it were a separate paragraph.

The Voice translation team decided it was important to reflect various literary styles throughout the version. We have seen this already in prose, dialogue, and acrostics. In the case of Philippians 2:6–11, the translators came up with a way of showing visually and rhythmically that poetry, not prose, undergirds Paul's admonition.

> Though He was in the form of God,
>   He chose not to cling to equality with God;
> But He poured Himself out *to fill a vessel brand new;*
>   a servant in form
>   and a man indeed.
> The very likeness of humanity.
> He humbled Himself,
>   obedient to death—
>   a merciless death on the cross!
> So God raised Him up to the highest place
>   and gave Him a name above all.
> So when His name is called,
>   every knee will bow,
>   in heaven, on earth, and below.
> And every tongue will confess
>   "Jesus, the Anointed One, is Lord,"
>   to the glory of God our Father!

This rendering represents true collaboration between scholars and writer-poets. The lines, rhythm, cadence, and supplied words clearly give the impression that these verses are not simply prose; they are a poem dedicated to rehearsing the master story of Jesus' career.

It was part of the mission of The Voice not only to capture the meaning of the text, but where possible to approximate the various

Contextual Equivalence in Practice

literary forms found in the Scriptures. This is not possible in every case, for the Hebrew and Greek contain wordplays, alliteration, assonance, and other features that cannot be represented in a second language. As scholars know, whenever you translate one language into another, something is lost; more often than not it is the form that is sacrificed. When possible The Voice team attempted to reproduce the literary form that shaped these ancient texts.

blog entry

July 12, 2012

"The Bogus World System"

by Jack Wisdom

We live in a rebellious and broken world. Even though God is the rightful owner of everything everywhere, there is a tragic gap between the way things are and the way things ought to be; the way things are is not the way God wants. That is why Jesus taught His followers to pray that God would "bring about [His] Kingdom" so that His will would be "manifest here on earth as it is manifest in heaven" (Matt. 6:10).

The New Testament describes this broken status quo in various ways, including the "world" (John 2:15), "this age" (Rom. 12:2), "this present evil age" (Gal. 1:4), and "the dominion of darkness" (Col. 1:13). The Voice uses a couple of descriptive phrases to translate the reality of our rebellious world. In multiple passages, for example, we find the phrase "this corrupt world order" (e.g., John 16:33). This phrase captures a deep and depressing theological fact—the shalom of God's good creation has been vandalized and corrupted by sin, and the status quo is "in the grips of the evil one" (1 John 5:19).

In James 4, the brother of Jesus comments on the violence that has shaped and continues to shape human history, and he chastises the readers (including us) for being unfaithful to God by "making friends with this corrupt world order" (James 4:4). James' point is clear: as followers of Jesus and citizens of God's Kingdom, we are called to be conscientious objectors to the disordered values and patterns of the "bogus world system."

I must confess that I had a vested personal interest in the team's decision to use the phrase "bogus world system" to describe the anti-shalomic disorder of the status quo. I wanted to see the phrase in print because—based on my own hazy recollection—I think I actually coined the phrase sometime in the 1980's when I was on Young Life staff. I recall that I was talking to some young men at Young Life's Frontier Ranch in Colorado. These guys had just become followers of Jesus, and they were concerned about going back to face "the real world." I challenged the idea that the so-called "real world" was somehow more real than the love they had experienced at Frontier Ranch, God's "powerful love revealed to us in a tangible display" on a Roman cross (Rom. 5:8). That love, I argued, is Reality. The so-called real world is really a bogus world system, which "already is wasting away, as are its selfish desires" (1 John 2:17). I challenged those guys to maintain that perspective, and by God's Spirit, to live with authenticity as agents of God's Kingdom in the midst of the bogus world system. That, of course, is easier said than done.

To live with authenticity, we must recognize that the bogus world system is bogus because of pride. C.S. Lewis identifies pride as "the essential vice, the utmost evil" and observes that "it was through pride that the devil became the devil. Pride leads to every other vice. It is the complete anti-God state of mind." The bogus world system is characterized and shaped by the "pompous sense of superiority" (1 John 2:16). All of us—each in his or her own way—are proud, and the consequences of our collective and personal pride are multifarious and tragic. That is the bad news.

The good news is that God has invaded the bogus world system, and—in a display of shocking humility—Jesus died on the cross to disarm the proud powers "who once ruled over us" (Col. 2:15). He invites us to shift our allegiance from the bogus world system to His Kingdom, but we must leave our pride behind. To enter God's Kingdom, we must imitate the King, we must get low.

The primary New Testament word usually translated "humble" literally refers to low-lying topography. In Classical Greek, the word was used metaphorically to describe low social position, and the servile, groveling behavior of low-class people in the class-conscious culture of ancient Greece. To say the least, the word did not have a positive connotation. In the New Testament, that perspective changes because the Kingdom of God turns the pride-based values of the bogus world system upside down. In Mary's song, she celebrates the coming of Jesus, who scatters the proud, topples the mighty, and exalts the lowly (Luke 1:31-52).

Nobody was ready for a Liberating King who was "gentle and humble of heart" (Matt. 11:29), but that is exactly what they got. His followers expected Him to lead a triumphant military struggle, and some of them actually were anticipating positions of status and power in the new regime, but Jesus had a radically different plan: "Unless you change and become like little children, you will never enter the kingdom of heaven. In that kingdom, the most humble . . . are the greatest" (Matt. 18:3-4).

When Jesus' words are heard in the context of First Century Judaism or Roman culture, rather than in the child-centric context of our own culture, it is clear that He was calling His followers to renounce all pretensions and delusions of greatness as defined by the bogus world system. He was not calling them to make themselves lower than they actually were, but to recognize where they really stood. That is why John Stott calls humility "nothing but the truth" and a "synonym for honesty."

After Jesus' death and resurrection, His followers gathered and sang praises to the One who "was in the form of God," but "humbled Himself, obedient to death—a merciless death on the cross" (Phil. 2:6-8). They joyfully sang that Jesus, because of His humility, had been given the Name above all, YHWH.

As conscientious objectors to the bogus world system, the first Christians encouraged one another to imitate Jesus by

"embrac[ing] true humility . . . and extend[ing] love to others"
(Phil. 2:3). This is foolishness in the eyes of the bogus world
system, but it is the way of the King and His Kingdom. Augustine
makes the point well: "Why are you so proud? God became
humble for your sake! Perhaps you would be ashamed to imitate
a humble man; then at least imitate a humble God. The Son of
God came as a man and became humble . . . Pride does its own
will; humility does the will of God."

Lord, give us the power and the wisdom to be conscientious objectors to the proud patterns of the bogus world system.
Teach us to get low, to be authentic agents of Your Kingdom in
the midst of the rebellious and broken status quo.[5]

These examples should be sufficient to show the kind of thought
and care that went into the process. Essentially, it was important
for all those on The Voice translation team to wrestle with two
contexts—the context of the ancient Scriptures and the context of
our modern readers—choosing the right words, supplying additional
commentary, and approximating literary styles to bridge the gap
between the two horizons. In fairness all translations must do this to
some degree, otherwise the version produced would be inaccessible.
Still The Voice translation team made it a strategic part of its process
in unprecedented ways.

chapter
6

The Divine Name

While many titles such as Lord, God, God-All-Powerful, and Commander are attributed to God in the Scripture, there is only one name by which God is to be known most clearly, the name revealed to Moses at Mt. Sinai. It occurs about six thousand times in the Old Testament in reference to the One True God of Israel. One of the important questions translation teams have to answer before they can move forward is, how do they translate this divine name and the other titles associated with God? The Voice translators and editorial team struggled with these issues and often did not agree. Still, in the end decisions have to be made on these relevant questions.

The transliteration of God's name from the Hebrew is *YHWH*. Although we don't know which vowels would have been pronounced with these four consonants, we think the name may best be brought over into English as *Yahweh*. Some translations today render the divine name as *Yahweh*,[1] but there are serious concerns about that. What if that is not the right spelling or pronunciation of God's holy name, a name protected by one of the Ten Commandments? What do we do about the sensibilities of true believers—particularly Jews—with regard to the name? Many Christian scholars today either refuse to use the name *Yahweh* or do so with the utmost care.

In the past some translators rendered the divine name Jehovah,[2] but this is actually a made-up name combining the consonants of *YHWH* (latinized to *JHVH*) with the vowel sounds of *Adonai*, one of the Hebrew words for "Lord." Today most Bible translations render the divine name as Lord. The capitalization of each letter signals the informed reader that the word refers to God's name and is not just a title of reverence and honor.

In The Voice we have taken special care to translate the divine name as "the Eternal One" or "the Eternal," depending on the narrative flow and context. The Voice is not the first Bible translation to render the divine name in this way. James Moffatt, Scottish minister and scholar, started to render the divine name *Yahweh* in his translation, but at the last minute he chose to follow Matthew Arnold and other French scholars who translated the name "the Eternal."[3] Moffatt's decision in no way influenced the way The Voice team regarded the question. Still it is helpful to know that The Voice is not the first major translation to render the divine name as "the Eternal." The decision was based upon a number of factors.

First, the name *YHWH* is clearly understood to be God's covenant name. It was revealed to Moses at Mt. Sinai:

> Moses: Let's say I go to the people of Israel and tell them, "The God of your fathers has sent me to *rescue* you," and then they reply, "What is His name?" What should I tell them then?
>
> Eternal One: I AM WHO I AM. This is what you should tell the people of Israel: "I AM has sent me to *rescue* you."
>
> This is what you are to tell Israel's people: "The Eternal One [*YHWH*], the God of your fathers, the God of Abraham, the God of Isaac, and the God of Jacob is the One who has sent me to you." This is My name forevermore, and this is the name by which all future generations shall remember Me. (Exodus 3:13–15)

The revelation of God's name to Moses is associated with two of the most important events in the Old Testament: the liberation of the Hebrew slaves from Egyptian bondage and the institution of God's covenant with Israel at Sinai. The declaration affirms that this God is none other than the God who had already appeared and established a covenant of blessing with Abraham and his sons. Therefore, it is a covenant name that links past, present, and future: I am the God who was with Abraham. I am the God who hears the prayers of My people now. I am the God who will rescue them in the future. I am the Eternal. It is a relational name that emphasizes God's saving actions and His "being there"—past, present, and future—for His covenant people.

Second, the name *YHWH* is built on the Hebrew verb meaning "to be" (*hayah*). When asked His name, God responds, "I AM WHO I AM." . . . [say] "I AM has sent me to rescue you." The verbal idea possesses a timeless quality. This is one reason why The Voice team thought the English word *eternal* helps to capture something of its meaning. Furthermore, God Himself emphasizes that this name is eternal; it stands forever and must be remembered by future generations of God's covenant partners.

While we have transliterated and anglicized most other names in Scripture (*Benyamin* = Benjamin; *Shemuel* = Samuel; *Yeshua* = Joshua; *Yeshayahu* = Isaiah; *Petros* = Peter; *Paulos* = Paul), we have chosen not to do so with the divine name out of respect for that name and our deep appreciation for both Jewish and Christian traditions. The Ten Directives warn against using the name of God in any frivolous, self-serving way: "You are not to use My name for your *own* idle purposes, for the Eternal will punish anyone who treats His name as anything less than sacred" (Exodus 20:7). Over time—and under the influence of this directive—faithful Jewish communities spoke the name less and less until it was prohibited from use altogether except on the most solemn occasions in the temple. Even when Scripture was read aloud in the synagogue, the readers did not utter the divine name; instead, when they came across it in the text, they substituted a word for it. In Aramaic-speaking synagogues they would say "*Adonai*";[4] in Greek-speaking synagogues they would say "*kyrios.*"

Scribes who copied the biblical books on the scrolls read in the synagogues often did not write the tetragrammaton, the four Hebrew

letters which make up the divine name. Among the biblical manuscripts of the Dead Sea Scrolls, the name was represented by four dots
above the line (• • • •) or it was written in archaic Hebrew script. This
would be like switching to a Gothic font when typing out the four
letters that make up the name YHWH. This made the name stand out
on the page so that readers would exercise care when they came to it.
Even letters that preceded the divine name were sometimes written in
this archaic script likely because they came in contact with the holy
name of God.

Many Jews today carry on this tradition of reverence by refus-
ing to speak the name at all and referring to God as *HaShem* ("the
name"). They extend the same consideration to the word *God* by
writing it without the vowel, *G-D*. Early Christians held similar
practices regarding sacred names and invented new ways to signal
that respect. When, for example, scribes wrote and copied the New
Testament books, they refrained from spelling out the names and
titles associated with God the Father, Son, and Spirit. Instead, they
employed what scholars call *nomina sacra*, or "sacred names." When
copyists came across these special names in the text, they would ab-
breviate them with two letters (generally) and draw a line above those
letters to indicate to the reader that this is a sacred name. Names such
as Jesus, God, and Holy Spirit are treated this way as well as titles such
as Anointed One, Lord, Son of God, and Son of Man.

The Voice's translation of the divine name by "the Eternal" and
"the Eternal One" carries on the church's long-standing tradition
of reverence for God and His name. It also attempts to translate the
meaning of the name and recontextualize it for contemporary culture. We wish to emphasize both the covenantal and eternal aspects of
God's name. It is covenantal in that God is revealing His special name
as a prelude to an enduring relationship with Him, a relationship in
which He promises to be there with and for us. It is eternal in that
God's name, like God Himself, is timeless and unchanging.

The decision to translate the divine name as "the Eternal" or
"the Eternal One" came several weeks after David Capes circulated

a memo to Chris Seay, Kelly Hall, Frank Couch, and Maleah Bell in July 2006. He was concerned at the time because the scholars, writers, and editorial team who were working through the psalms had come up with a variety of ways for translating the name and titles of God. It was apparent that some decision needed to be made to standardize the names before the work progressed any further.

Capes queried the scholars working on the project regarding the question. Although there was no consensus on what to do, there was broad agreement that (1) it was an important issue that needed to be decided and (2) the editorial team needed to be consistent throughout the Old Testament. It was also advised that somewhere in the front matter of the translation that the editors lay out the decisions and the theological rationales.

Some of the scholars advised the editors to render the divine name either YHWH (unvocalized Hebrew name) or Yahweh (vocalized Hebrew name). They argued that not only was it accurate but that postmodern audiences were accustomed to unusual names and would not find it strange. They pointed to the Harry Potter series and the Lord of the Rings trilogy as an example of recent literature in which unusual names were typical. Other scholars urged us to exercise caution and not employ the divine name (YHWH or Yahweh) in this translation out of respect for the name and how Christian tradition has handled it in the past. In the end, the team decided not to transliterate the divine name as *Yahweh* but to translate it as "the Eternal."

Elohim

Most Bible translations render the Hebrew word *Elohim* as "God" when referring to the God of Israel or "gods" when referring to heavenly powers or pagan gods. The Hebrew word has a broad-enough range of meaning to be used for either. At the heart of the word is a sense of power, authority, and divinity. The ending on the word indicates it is plural, which is typically understood as a plural of majesty when referring to the One God of Israel; it does not indicate that the Hebrew Scriptures understand Israel's God either as one of many gods or as a triune God as He is understood in later Christian theology.

The problem with the English word *God* is that it does not always carry a particular meaning. In the ancient world there were many god options. Every tribe or nation had its gods. In a Roman city there could be a temple dedicated to a different god on nearly every corner. In the Roman market every guild or profession had an image of the god that superintended the craft in their stalls. Though the modern world is somewhat different, in many ways the word *God* still carries little-to-no specific meaning. The Hindu religion talks about millions of gods. Muslims confess "there is no God but Allah." The question "Do you believe in God?" is meaningless until you answer the question "Which God are you referring to?" So it is important to be as specific as possible when talking about God.

Typically in Bible translations, the capitalized form is used to refer to the One True God of Abraham, Isaac, and Jacob, while the lowercase form is used to refer to the so-called deities worshiped by Israel's neighbors, that is, gods that are not gods at all. The Voice translation team decided to translate *Elohim* as "God" or "True God" when referring to the One God of Israel and "god" or "gods" depending on context when referring to pagan gods or heavenly powers. This provides some specificity. Accordingly, "God" or "True God" refers not to a no-name deity but to a specific God who engaged the people of Israel in a special, covenantal relation, a God identified by name as YHWH. Furthermore, when it comes to the New Testament, this same God is God the Father of the Lord Jesus, the Anointed, who adopts as His own all who commit themselves to Jesus. This is why true believers can boldly pray, "Our Father in heaven."

Adonai

Most translations will render *Adonai* "Lord." Note that *-ord* is in the lower case to distinguish this title from the rendering of the divine name. Sometimes it is translated as "master," "lord," or "sir" when referring to authorities such as kings or slave owners. At the heart of this word is the recognition that someone is in authority over another, be it a king over a citizen, a husband over a wife, or a master over a slave. The key issue is authority. This title often occurs in combination with other titles: *Adonai YHWH* or *Adonai Elohim.*

The Voice translation team opted for a traditional translation of this word. When referring to the God of Israel, they translated it "Lord," "Master," or "God." When referring to human authorities, they used "lord," "sir," or "master." There are also a few places where *Baal* refers to the God of Israel. In those cases, we translated it "Master" or "Lord." Most occurrences of this word, however, refer to another deity worshiped by the Canaanites.

YHWH Sabaoth

One phrase that is notoriously difficult to translate involves a combination of YHWH and a Hebrew title, *Sabaoth.* Most modern versions simply translate God's name as "Lord" and then transliterate the Hebrew title into English. The result is the combination, "Lord Sabaoth." That may work for other translations, but The Voice translation team was not satisfied to transliterate titles like this. After all "Lord Sabaoth" sounds like a character in *Star Wars:* "Lord Sabaoth, the death star is ready."

When you consider the meaning of the divine name and the title Sabaoth, you discover a number of important connections. With these in mind, we decided to translate the combination of name and title this way: "The Eternal, Commander of heavenly armies."

As we noticed above, the meaning of God's name is best captured by the English adjectival noun, "the Eternal" or "the Eternal One." The name is derived from the Hebrew verb "to be" and implies the one who is, who was, and who is to come.

The title Sabaoth is sometimes rendered "hosts," but that is not a meaningful way of understanding it these days. We discussed the translation at length, finally deciding on the phrase "Commander of heavenly armies." Clearly the title implies that God is in charge, but His "in-chargeness" in this age is imperfect on this earth. That is why this world is so badly broken, why Jesus urged His followers to pray that God's will be done on earth as it is in heaven, and why the New Testament teaches that the risen Lord will one day return to finish what He started two thousand years ago.

Only in heaven are God's commands heeded fully, without compromise. People disobey God's good and reasonable directives every day here on earth. So the Scriptures—both Old and New—imply that there is a heavenly army at God's command. You see, evil, when it is defeated, will not go easily; it will not give up without a fight. While some are uncomfortable with the Bible's military metaphors and anticipation of a violent end to evil, we must be careful not to sweep them away or attempt to translate them out of existence. We must take them seriously and learn from them how deeply entrenched evil is in us and in this bogus world around us. When real evil is upon you, you pray for something or someone more powerful to come and liberate you. This is the root meaning of the word *Sabaoth*: an army or force capable of stopping evil.

Consider what has happened in Syria in 2011 and 2012. As hundreds and thousands of Syrians laid in the rubble of formerly glorious cities injured and dying at the hands of the brutal Assad regime, many in Damascus took to Twitter, the Internet, and social media to plead for help. How would they hope that help would come? In some force more powerful than the cruel forces oppressing them.

Similarly at the end of World War II, allied forces marched into Europe to the cheers and applause of people who lived for years under the heel of the SS and Nazi oppression. The sight of the victorious army brought joy and delight to people in places we will never know.

Those of us who live in relative safety of the West would urge the Syrians to be patient and wait for a diplomatic solution, and all the while they are maimed, dismembered, raped, and killed. For much of biblical history, the people of the covenants—Jews and Christians alike—suffered terribly under brutal regimes of Assyrians, Babylonians, Greeks, and Romans. They were persecuted, displaced, robbed, separated from their loved ones, and living in fear for their lives. The image of God as a "Commander of heavenly armies" offered them hope that one day God would bring them relief from their hardships.

The book of Revelation describes a day when Jesus will return, mounted on a white steed and surrounded by the heavenly army. The King of all kings and Lord of all lords will command the final battle. On that day history as we know will come to an end, and evil—in all of its twisted and distorted manifestations—will be met and defeated, finally, decisively.

Pronouns

Joe Hackman of Hackman's Bible Bookstore in Allentown, Pennsylvania, put together an event for area pastors and church leaders to hear about The Voice translation in May 2012. After Frank Couch and I introduced The Voice and did a few readings, we took questions from the audience. A woman pastor asked a very good question: "Why did you use masculine pronouns to refer to God?" Well, that was the first time the two of us had heard that question. I'd like to say that I offered a brilliant answer, but frankly I didn't. So I went back home and gave the question more thought.

When it comes to pronouns, English provides three options: masculine, feminine, and neuter. It is either God . . . He or God . . . She or God . . . It. The Voice translation team ruled out the third option because *it* is used with impersonal not personal antecedents. In natural speech English-speakers don't use *it* to refer to persons; they use *it* to refer to things. Remember the theme of the project is built around the idea of "the voice" that has spoken and continues to speak. Things might make a sound, but they don't have a voice. Only a person has a voice, and the Christian Scriptures are clear that God is not an impersonal force or thing; God is a person. So we are left with two options: *he* or *she*.

99

When you look at the original Greek, Hebrew, and Aramaic texts, the pronouns used to refer to God are masculine. Likewise many of the metaphors used to refer to God are masculine. God is referred to as "Father," "King," "Warrior," and "Shepherd." These are masculine words and images. Now this is not to say that God is male in the sense that roughly half the human population is male. In fact, Genesis 1:27 makes it clear that God's image in humanity includes both maleness and femaleness: "So God did *just that*. He created humanity in His image, created them male and female." So males have no more claim on God's image than females. Both equally share God's relational richness and image.

Still we, as translators, are left with a choice: Do we use masculine pronouns or feminine to refer to God? Some scholars on the project urged us to use both. According to their recommendation, one sentence might read, "God . . . He"; the next would say, "God . . . She." But the editorial team was concerned that this would only lead to confusion. Still other scholars advised that we do away with any pronouns when referring to God. But the team was concerned that this direction would lead to redundancy and make the translation difficult to read. Pronouns are very useful!

In the end the decision was made to use masculine pronouns in reference to God because (1) it reflects the original texts, (2) it is consistent with many of the images and metaphors used to refer to God, (3) it is consistent with the Christian tradition, and (4) it leads to less confusion. Not everyone will be happy with that decision. In fact, some of the translators and scholars who worked on the project were not happy with it. But when we looked at the overall project, we felt it was the best way to deal with a difficult question.

As we talked to many women in our target audience of eighteen- to thirty-five-year old adults, we discovered that they were not concerned or bothered by referring to God as "He." While some in society claim that violence against women and the poor treatment of women can be traced to the perceived "maleness" of the God of the Bible, our intended audience did not share those concerns. They appear to understand the limits of language. They appreciate the fact that the Bible was written at a time and in a culture far different than our own. They do not think that we today stand in some superior moral or spiritual place in regard to these issues. They realize that our culture is broken and our lives are messy. They do not feel excluded or second class to men by reading of God in these masculine terms.

Clearly, these are tough issues. The Voice editorial team struggled with them knowing that whatever decision they made would not suit everyone.

Capitalization

Finally, the editorial team decided to capitalize all names, titles, and pronouns associated with God, Jesus, and the Holy Spirit. This decision was based on a number of factors. First, by capitalizing the various names and titles for the triune God, The Voice stands in continuity with other modern translations. This extends to capitalizing the key words in phrases such as Son of David, Son of God, and Son of Man. Second, by capitalizing titles and pronouns associated with all three persons of the Trinity, The Voice signals a commitment by Thomas Nelson, Inc., and Ecclesia Bible Society to orthodox Christian teaching as summarized in the creeds: "we believe in God the Father . . . God the Son . . . God the Holy Spirit." Finally, by capitalizing even the pronouns referring to the persons of the Trinity, The Voice departs from recent trends in biblical translations in which divine pronouns are not capitalized. The capitalization of the pronouns acknowledges the long tradition in the church of representing her faith in the Trinity through material culture. Just as Christian scribes and iconographers signaled their devotion by using *nomina sacra* in Christian manuscripts and icons, so The Voice team signifies its devotion by capitalizing all pronouns associated with God, Jesus, and the Holy Spirit.

chapter 7

The Product Line

When John Eames and Chris Seay put together the initial proposal
for what would become The Voice Bible, they recommended to the
publishers a series of trade books that would be released on the way
to publishing the entire Bible. This plan was patterned in some ways
on the various releases associated with the publication of Eugene
Peterson's translation, *The Message: The Bible in Contemporary
Language.* NavPress released various sections of The Message over a
nine-year period:

- The New Testament (1993)
- The Old Testament Wisdom Literature (1998)
- The Hebrew Prophets (2000)
- The Pentateuch (2001)
- The Historical Books (2002)
- The Full Bible (2002)

The success of The Message in the market inspired Chris and
John to follow a similar path. The initial proposal for what was then
called "The Word: The Divine Utterance of The Creators (Known
Historically as the Bible)" forecast the entire project could be completed in four years. Here are the products they proposed initially
along with their projected release dates:

The Book of Jesus	October 2005
The Book of the Church	April 2006
The Book of Paul	October 2006
The New Testament	April 2007
The Book of Songs	October 2007
The Great People of God	April 2008
The Bible	October 2008

"The Book of Jesus" was to be centered on the four New Testament Gospels. The proposal described this book as follows: "The life of Jesus has reshaped the course of human history. From His miraculous birth to His brutal execution His life and teachings are without parallel."

"The Book of the Church" was to begin in the Gospels, but its trajectory would have taken it to the Acts of the Apostles and early church history. Here is how this trade book was envisioned: "The story of Christ is made complete in the object of God's affection, the historical community of believers known as His church. From it's [sic] inception as a band of renegades led by bickering Apostles to the spattering of modern day denominations the grace of Christ is still made known by His bride."

"The Book of Paul" would have told the remarkable story of Paul beginning with Luke's portrayal of Saul the Pharisee in the Acts of the Apostles and then incorporating the texts of the thirteen letters written under his name. Chris imagined the book this way: "An arrogant and cold-blooded killer is chosen by God to lead the advancement of the church. Enter the mind of this adventurous leader as he cares for the gentiles he previously despised."

"The Book of Songs" would have been the first book in the series to deal with the Old Testament. Since the book of Psalms was the hymnal of the early church, Chris was advocating a return to the psalms with new melodies to ignite and invigorate the church as believers gathered in worship. He planned to bring together the best songwriters and worship leaders he could enlist to assist in translating these songs and return them to their place of prominence in the body of Christ. In addition to the psalms, this book would have

103

incorporated other biblical stories and the songs associated with them, for example the song composed following the exodus in Exodus 15, Deborah's song in Judges 5, and the Magnificat in Luke 2. Through the biblical songs the entire sweep of salvation can be told. There were some discussions in these early days as well—but never put in writing—about the possibility of music being written and recorded as part of The Voice project. At the time, these notions remained vague, but within two years songwriters and musicians would be in the studio.

"The Great People of God" was proposed as a trade book that began in Genesis with the story of Abraham, the father of God's covenant people. Over time the Scriptures offer a mixed account. There are seasons when the people of God are heroic and faithful, but there are others when treachery and disloyalty characterize their journey. Chris envisioned a book that would tell the whole messy truth and reveal the checkered past of God's deeply flawed people. But once again, it was through these people that God intended to redeem the world.

In addition to these trade books, Chris also discussed another that he called "The Book of Wisdom": "This letter from a father to his son is blunt, practical, and insightful. James McDonald, a consummate father and Pastor, will recapture the most practical book in the cannon [sic]."

The Best-Laid Plans

By the time the contracts were signed between Chris Seay of Ecclesia Bible Society and World Publishing, the publisher had accepted in principle the release of several trade books on the way to the publication of the full Bible. But over time, the titles and descriptions of these products changed. In addition, as things happened, the four years slipped into seven before the full Bible could be published.

The Last Eyewitness
The first book published in The Voice project was *The Last Eyewitness: The Final Week*.[1] This hardback book describes the last week

in the life of Jesus told primarily from the standpoint of John (John 13—21). According to tradition, he was the "beloved disciple" and last eyewitness to Jesus. If so, he would have been the last person on earth to remember what Jesus looked like or to have heard the sound of His voice. Alan Culpepper and David Capes assisted Chris with his work on John's Gospel. The commentary was written in the first person, as if John himself—an old man by now—were telling the story. The book also includes excerpts from the passion narratives of Matthew, Mark, and Luke as retold by other writers and scholars. In later editions that include the entire Gospel of John, these notes are altered to take on the same style as the other Gospels and are spread throughout the Gospel rather than all appearing in the last nine chapters. The quotes from Matthew, Mark, and Luke are eliminated. In *The Last Eyewitness* the reader is invited to enter into the story, a theme that helped set the direction of the rest of The Voice project: "This unique work captures the urgency of the last living disciple telling his students about the most significant event in history. . . . The compelling story gives the reader the sense of being around a campfire with first century believers, hearing the story directly from John. So come into the story, smell the mixture of the salty air and billows of smoke floating from the bonfire and hear the Last Eyewitness."[2]

Something else that set this book apart from later products in The Voice line were seventeen dramatic illustrations by London-based artist Rob Pepper. Pepper utilizes a technique that he calls *conscious reflex drawing* to portray the world around him. In employing this method Pepper does not look at the paper while drawing; instead he fixes his attention on the object itself. This technique keeps the hand moving and consciously responding in the moment, rather than being influenced by the interplay between mind and eye. Because of this, Pepper's drawings invite a fresh perspective that liberates the work from any optical preconceptions or other visual judgments. Conscious reflex drawing enables the artist to capture the real essence of a situation or a moment.

The drawings in *The Last Eyewitness* are part of a wider series of artwork known as the Doxology series. Pepper created them by viewing some of the masterworks from the Christian tradition in London churches and museums. He drew some of these images during worship services in the company of believers, others when he was alone under candlelight. Still others he composed while standing among the crowds in the National Gallery in London. These simple, yet elegant depictions ornament the book and enhance the story of the last eyewitness.

In order to promote *The Last Eyewitness* and The Voice project, Thomas Nelson organized "The Last Eyewitness Tour" during Holy Week 2006. The tour featured the art of Rob Pepper, music from The Robbie Seay Band and Don and Lori Chaffer of Waterdeep, and experiential teaching from author and pastor Chris Seay. The tour stopped and led worship in the cities and venues across eastern and midwestern North America:

April 7	Tyndale College, Toronto, Ontario
April 8–9	Willow Creek Community Church, South Barrington Hills, Illinois
April 10	Windsor Crossing Community Church, Chesterfield, Missouri
April 11	The People's Church, Nashville, Tennessee
April 12	The Point, Snellville, Georgia
April 13	The University of Kentucky, Lexington, Kentucky
April 14	First Presbyterian Church, Pine Bluff, Arkansas

One participant described the event this way: "The night is an alternative worship time with music, teaching, communion, original film, and art. Each of the artists/speakers has unique abilities that they are combining with the goal of engaging and preparing people for Easter with the story of Jesus, through the eyes of the apostle John." Since the story told in the book *The Last Eyewitness* has to do with the final week in Jesus' life, the Holy Week tour provided an appropriate setting for not only engaging Scripture but also debuting the new translation.

blog entry

June 16, 2012

A Londoner at the Astros Game

by David Capes

When Chris Seay started Ecclesia, he had a great idea. He purchased Houston Astros season tickets in the upper deck of Minute Maid Park and would use the opportunity to connect with new and old friends. Church growth via 81 home games and America's favorite pastime. The idea worked well. A number of lives have been changed forever as the Killer B's (Biggio, Bagwell, and Berkman) rounded the bases and headed for home.

The very first product in The Voice Bible project was a book several of us worked on entitled *The Last Eyewitness: The Final Week.* There is a tradition that John, one of Jesus' twelve, outlived all the other disciples and became the last person on earth who had seen Jesus of Nazareth as He traveled the Galilean hills preaching, teaching, and healing. He was the last eyewitness to the life of Jesus, the last person to remember the look of His face and the sound of His voice.

The book told the story of the last week of Jesus' life. It was written in the first person, told from the perspective of an old man (John) who wanted to pass down to his own disciples the key events of that fateful week.

The Last Eyewitness is one of my favorite products in The Voice project because of the artwork of Rob Pepper. Rob is a Londoner who has a unique style of drawing; it is simple yet elegant. With just a few lines drawn in ink, highlighted with a minimal amount of metallic gold, Pepper provides our book with 17 dramatic illustrations of Jesus' life. These illustrations were

107

themselves inspired by great masterworks of Christian art. They add a great deal to the tone and texture of the book.

The first time I met Rob was at an Astros game—courtesy of Chris Seay—on a warm, clear night in Houston. Because it was not a hot day in the Bayou city, the roof was back which gave us a wonderful view not only of the field but of the Houston skyline.

Rob did not know baseball. But like any good Londoner he knew cricket, so we spent about half the game talking baseball—history, strategy, etc.—comparing it to cricket (You see, I had spent 7 months in Edinburgh, Scotland on sabbatical in 2000; so I knew a bit about cricket).

It was a good night of baseball for the Houston Astros. A lot of runs were scored and the Astros came out on top. Rob learned a little about a quintessential American experience, a night at a baseball game.

But it was what happened in the 7th inning that sticks out most in my mind about that night. Rob took out paper and pen and began to sketch the lines and contours of the baseball park from our vantage high above the field. I had become a fan of his during the project and was frankly amazed at the way he was able to capture the world around him with minimal lines and emphases. He went on to finish the piece and named it "The Juice Bowl," a reference to the fact that Enron Field had recently been renamed Minute Maid Park.

The Voice Bible project has brought together some amazing people with enormous talents. We gathered writers, artists, musicians, poets, scholars, and editors to do a project which will never be done again. It has been a unique—or as the Brits would say—"a one-off" experience.

Often, I've learned, the most meaningful moments in life come when you least expect it but most need it. Meeting Rob that night, hearing his story and seeing him at work provided me—and others I'm sure—with some much-needed inspiration.[3]

The Voice CDs

Two of the earliest products released as part of The Voice project were music CDs inspired by The Voice translation. As indicated earlier, it was Chris's intention all along to return the biblical psalms to a place of prominence in contemporary worship. In keeping with this, *Songs from The Voice, Vol. 1* contained thirteen original songs written by various artists inspired by the translations from The Voice project.[4] The title cut, "Please Don't Make Us Sing This Song," was written and performed by Lori Chaffer. It reflects the themes and sentiments of Psalm 137, a lament written against the backdrop of great tragedy in Israel. The song was recorded about the time that Hurricane Katrina slammed into the Gulf Coast, leaving behind unimaginable death and destruction. Film-makers wed Lori's version of Psalm 137 with video footage from New Orleans to express our national grief and record the moment for future generations. The first Voice CD was produced and mixed by Lori's husband, Don Chaffer. Sandra McCracken, Sara Groves, Derek Webb, Seth Woods, the Robbie Seay Band, and other artists contributed. The music was recorded at The Culture House Studios in Olathe, Kansas. Hank Williams mastered the tracks at Mastermix in Nashville, Tennessee.

Five months later, a second CD was released entitled *Son of the Most High*.[5] Produced by Don Chaffer and engineered by Russ Long, this CD included twelve original songs based on The Voice translation of key scriptures found in the libretto of Handel's *Messiah*. Don Chaffer, Lori Chaffer, Jill Paquette, Tara Leigh Cobble, Matt Wertz, and dozens of other writers and musicians again recorded the music at The Culture House Studios in Olathe, Kansas. Hank Williams also mastered this recording at Mastermix in Nashville, Tennessee.

Several of the songs from these CDs were included with the publication of a trade paperback, *The Voice from On High*.

The Dust Off Their Feet: Lessons from the First Church and *The Voice of Luke: Not Even Sandals*

In 2006 Thomas Nelson released *The Dust Off Their Feet*.[6] It is described as "The Book of Acts Retold by Brian McLaren." Darrell Bock and David Capes assisted Brian with the translation. Devotional commentary written by David, Brian, and Chris is scattered throughout, clearly distinguished from the text of Acts itself in the formatting. At the end of the book are essays written by pastors and church leaders divided into two sections: (1) "The Evolving Church in Acts" and (2) "The Evolving Church of Today." Contributors included Robert Creech, Greg Garrett, Andrew Jones, Tim Keel, Evan Lauer, Kerry Shook, Chuck Smith Jr., and David Capes.

The cover of the book—designed by Scott Lee Designs—won the 2007 Evangelical Christian Publishers Association Book Cover Design Award in the Bible category. It features a picture of the soles of a man's feet. The feet are gnarly and covered in mud; they have clearly seen many miles, many hardships, and many adventures. The image—as well as the title to the book—are meant to recall Jesus' instructions to His disciples when He sends them out to liberate the oppressed, heal the sick, and proclaim the kingdom in His name: "If a town rejects you, shake the dust from your feet as you leave as a witness against them" (Luke 9:5). But the image also anticipates the cover to one of the next books in the series, *The Voice of Luke: Not Even Sandals.*[7]

The cover to that book has a picture of a man's bare feet seen from behind as he walks on bare dirt. The feet are dirty but not caked in mud as in the previous cover image. What is clear is that these feet are beautiful because they are bringing the good news (Romans 10:15, quoting Isaiah 52:7). But they are sandal-less because at one point Jesus had sent His followers out with only the shirts on their back: "No, Peter, the truth is that before the rooster crows at dawn, you will have denied that you even know Me, not just once, but three times. Remember when I sent you out with no money, no pack, not even sandals? Did you lack anything?" (Luke 22:35). Brian McLaren served as the primary writer and translator to *The Voice of Luke*, reviewed and supplemented by Darrell Bock and David Capes. In the front matter, Ecclesia Bible Society indicates why Brian was the right person to work with Luke's Gospel:

Choosing Brian McLaren to retell his [Luke's] story was not a difficult decision. His writing style is clearly similar to Luke's. The attention given to detail, the awareness of contemporary culture, and the role of the Gentile church are paralleled in Brian's work. Brian McLaren best represents the refined physician who documented the history of Jesus and those who pioneered the church.

As with earlier products in The Voice series, devotional notes are scattered through the book in appropriate places in the story. Differences in background and formatting distinguish carefully the text of Luke's Gospel from these commentary sections. The commentary itself represents a collaborative effort between Brian McLaren and David Capes to offer the reader insights into the culture, history, and contemporary relevance of the Scriptures.

The Voice of Matthew

The Voice of Matthew[8] is a unique retelling of the life of Jesus from the perspective of a Jewish believer who wants to connect the past with the future. Since Matthew's Gospel is the most Jewish Gospel, it made sense to assign the task to Lauren Winner, a woman with significant life experience in the company of Jews. Peter Davids and David Capes took care of the scholarly review and recommendations for this book. Lauren and David collaborated on the commentary embedded, but carefully delineated, throughout the Gospel. *The Voice of Matthew* reads like a novel with fascinating gems scattered throughout, providing the careful reader with one of the most satisfying Bible-reading experiences ever.

blog entry

November 28, 2012

A Remarkable Day

by David Capes

As I look back over the journey we've been on with The Voice project, there are a number of moments that stand out. One of those happened in 2004 when Chris Seay and I boarded an early morning flight to Nashville for what would turn out to be a remarkable day.

I don't recall the exact sequence of events on landing, but I remember soon being in a van with several people I had never met. They had already begun work translating and working on the Gospels. We headed south out of Nashville. The van was filled with animated conversations, new people being introduced, old friends connecting again after a long time. There was an air of excitement and expectation. We were embarking on something new, for all of us.

We arrived about an hour later at the home of Frank Couch. I had heard of Frank but had never met him. Frank is an iconic figure in publishing at Thomas Nelson. He knows everyone and everyone knows him. He also knows more about publishing Bibles than anyone on the planet. I didn't know it at the time—we seldom do—but Frank was destined to become a good friend and mentor to me through this project. Without Frank's knowledge, energy, focus, and commitment to The Voice and what it stood for, I dare say we would never have made it.

We enjoyed a brief tour of Frank's home. The setting is beautiful there in the rugged hills of Middle Tennessee. Frank, I learned, had built the house himself. Because I know something of construction, I was amazed as I looked around to see what he and his wife had dreamed up and built together. It is a wonderful and warm home.

After the tour we settled down on the deck and began to talk about where we were heading on this journey together. Chris's literary agent, John Eames, joined us. John had worked with Eugene Peterson in publishing The Message. Others from Thomas Nelson gathered with us.

As one just recently brought into the conversation, I listened intently. Life has taught me to do more listening than talking in situations like that. I knew I was surrounded by some amazing and gifted people, people deeply committed to the Scriptures and to the church.

At one moment in that conversation—a moment which even now seems a bit magical—we sat quietly and listened to the suggested translation of Matthew chapter 1. Now this is a chapter most people skip over. In the KJV it is referred to as the "begat" chapter. It is a long genealogy of names in Jesus' family line, names that seem pretty remote to us. But if you know the Hebrew Scriptures—like Matthew's original audience no doubt did—you know that behind each name is a story. For those of us who don't know these Old Testament characters well, the new translation fills in some of the gaps. By the time we got to Mary and the birth of Jesus we were set up to hear something very special.

The sound of Scripture read aloud against the warm Tennessee breeze had a soothing effect on me and everyone in the circle. It had been a hectic day—an early morning flight, meeting new people, a bit of nervousness about this project we had all agreed to work on but nobody exactly understood. When the reading was completed, everyone remained quiet. No one wanted to interrupt the providential silence. In that moment I think we all experienced a moment of clarity about what we were about.

113 *The Product Line*

We left Nashville the next day in a flurry of handshakes and hugs, with promises to be in touch. But we left with a clearer sense of where this journey was taking us. It had been a remarkable day—a day I look back on fondly—because it set the pace and agenda for much of what would follow.[9]

The Voice from On High

One of the best-known choral oratorios in history is Georg Friedrich Handel's *Messiah* (1742). *The Voice from On High* was inspired by Handel's masterpiece and libretto composed by Charles Jennens. This unique Voice product draws from the same Scripture portions quoted by Jennens and tells the story of the long-awaiting Messiah, the Liberating King, Jesus. Beginning with creation and moving through Revelation, *The Voice from On High* brings together some of the most memorable passages from the Old and New Testaments. The book tells the story of creation and salvation as if it were a grand oratorio composed and performed on the stage of the universe.

> An eternal song is playing. Before the first flash of light interrupted the darkness, it was there. Before the first tug of gravity pulled the heavenly bodies into a celestial dance, it filled the cosmos. Before raging waters carved deep valleys through rock mountains, it thundered like a waterfall. The Bible bears witness to this song that tells the story of the one True God— the Creator, Composer, and Conductor of the great oratorio of redemption. In each movement we hear the music that changes the world forever.[10]

The book is beautifully formatted and contains various images of musical instruments. It was written for the express purpose of being part of a complete multisensory experience. A CD containing seven songs from the first two Voice CDs complements the book. People are invited to put on their headphones, read the book, contemplate the art, and hear the Voice of the One True God.

The Voice Revealed

In *The Voice Revealed: The True Story of the Last Eyewitness*,[11] Chris Seay completes the translation of John's Gospel begun with the publication of *The Last Eyewitness*. The story is supplemented with commentary throughout written in the first person, as if John himself were the one telling it. As with *The Last Eyewitness*, Alan Culpepper and David Capes assisted Chris with the translation.

The Voice of Hebrews

Long before The Voice project began, it started as an idea in the mind of Chris Seay. That idea was nurtured in the company of friends, one of whom was Greg Garrett. Greg is the author of the critically acclaimed novels *Free Bird* and *Cycling*. At the time of publication he was professor of English at Baylor University and writer-in-residence at the Episcopal Theological Seminary of the Southwest in Austin, Texas. Greg and Chris had coauthored the book entitled *The Gospel Reloaded*, so he had already worked with and encouraged Chris along this journey for years. Now with the release of *The Voice of Hebrews: The Mystery of Melchizedek*, Greg's first book-length contribution to the series was made.[12] David Capes worked with Greg on the translation and composed the commentary throughout. That commentary is delineated carefully from the text of Hebrews itself.

The subtitle, "The Mystery of Melchizedek," comes from an extended commentary in chapter 7 regarding the priest-king Melchizedek, one of the most enigmatic figures in all the Scriptures. David attempted to amplify the voice of the anonymous author of this early Christian letter by explaining what we know about Melchizedek and linking him to Jesus, the Liberating King. The book's remarkable cover—designed by Scott Lee Designs—features the face of a bearded man, dressed as one might imagine a king might be three thousand years ago. A homeless man agreed to serve as the model for the image; he was discovered living on the streets of Nashville. Like Melchizedek, where he came from and where he was headed remains a mystery.

blog entry

August 16, 2012

A Memorable Cover: The Voice of Hebrews

by Scott Lee

I was walking downtown one day and came across this homeless guy on the sidewalk and thought he looked like a great old, biblical character. Since I knew we were working on the cover to *The Voice of Hebrews: The Mystery of Melchizedek,* I thought it would be a great idea to shoot him as a model and use him on one of the proposed cover designs. You see, when a publisher hires a design agency to create a book cover, the agency sends them a lot of comps (proposed designs) to choose from. I asked him if he would be interested in wearing a costume and letting me shoot some pictures of him for a book cover, for money of course, and he said, "You bet!"

We decided on a time and place to meet to shoot the pictures, so I went and rented a costume, drove back to where we agreed to meet and he actually showed up! I explained the project to him, what the book was about and the concept behind the whole Voice line of products, then shot a ton of photos of him. I paid him his money, told him thanks, and agreed that I would come back when the book was printed to give him a copy.

When I received the printed books, I took a couple and drove back downtown to where we had met and tried to find him, but to no avail. I even went over to a little convenience store nearby thinking the owner may know who he was since he probably came in often. They knew him and told me where he usually sleeps. So, I drove over to the place they told me he camps (that place was scary); but I couldn't find him anywhere. Unfortunately I was never able to connect with him again to give him a copy of the book. It was a great experience though, even if I was never able to close the story well.[13]

blog entry

A Few Days in Austin

by David Capes

Most of our collaboration on The Voice took place by means of technology: through email, Internet, SKYPE, and cell phones. In some cases the work was personal, that is, people knew and worked closely with their reviewers and commentators. In other cases, the work together was anonymous. It is standard practice in scholarly work for a person's book or article to be reviewed anonymously, so neither the writers nor the reviewers know the identity of the other. This process ensures that a person's feelings—positively or negatively—about another do not affect the quality of the review. I understood the need for those checks and balances.

But there were a few remarkable occasions when writers and scholars actually sat down together, face-to-face, to work through a translation.

One of my favorite times working on The Voice project took place in Austin, TX. Greg Garrett, a noted novelist and nonfiction writer, was working on the translation of the book of Hebrews, so I drove over to spend a few days with him. It was summer, so he had arranged for us to work in empty classrooms at the Episcopal Theological Seminary of the Southwest, the institution where he had studied for his Master of Divinity degree and would later remain as writer-in-residence. The staff of the school graciously allowed me to stay in one of the dorm rooms—on The Voice discount of course.

Over the next few days, Greg and I shared meals, swapped stories, and settled down over the Greek text of the letter to the Hebrews. I watched carefully and listened closely as Greg, a gifted writer, worked through the challenging prose of one of the New Testament's most sophisticated and difficult-to-translate books. We plotted the argument and puzzled over the best way to communicate to our modern audience the way our anonymous Jewish author went about persuading his Jewish audience about the superiority of God's new covenant. I remember watching Greg count out the syllables—the rhythm—of the prose. I learned from watching Greg that well-crafted prose has a rhythm; meter is not restricted to poetry. I had never thought of it before, but working with Greg convinced me it was true.

Scholars are often strongly left-brained people; this means they are good on the technicalities. A translator might say, "This word is a Greek adverbial concessive participle and its referent is thus-and-so" or "This syllable is a pronominal suffix on the Hebrew root and its antecedent is x-y-z." Scholars can do that sort of thing all day long. But gifted writers, poets, and artists are often strong right-brained people. They are better equipped than technical scholars at capturing the beauty of a phrase or finding the right word to resolve the rhythm of a poem. This is why I'm fond of saying about The Voice, "Finally, a Bible for both sides of your brain!"

I remember leaving Austin on the last day a bit sad. Greg and I had run out of time, and we had not been able to translate through all 13 chapters of this tough letter. We would have to go back to our respective lives to complete it, in between other duties. I was sad too that more of my Voice-related experience had been so isolated. Translation is often a solitary experience—the nature of the discipline demands it be so—even if you are working in a "collaborative environment." As I started the car and headed for home, I was grateful for Greg's talent and friendship. When I look back, those were good days.[14]

The Voice of Mark

Greg Garrett's second contribution to The Voice project was released only a few months later. In *The Voice of Mark: Let Them Listen*,[15] Greg retells the story of Jesus as found in Mark's Gospel, likely the first New Testament Gospel written. Compared to Matthew, Luke, and John, Mark's account of Jesus' life is raw and fast-paced. It is hard to walk away from this Gospel without being forced to deal with two crucial questions: "Who is the Son of Man?" and "What should I do in light of His most remarkable life, death, and resurrection?" Peter Davids and David Capes worked with Greg to fine-tune the translation. Matthew Paul Turner complements the text of Mark with commentary that explains relevant historical, cultural, and spiritual features of the Gospel. Turner is the former editor of CCM (Christ-Community-Music) magazine and author of several books.

The Voice of Romans

Although another writer had contracted originally to depict the voice of Paul in the New Testament, that task eventually fell to a team of three writers: Chris Seay, Kelly Hall, and David Capes. Together they worked through the thirteen letters written under Paul's name. The first installment of the work on Paul was published as *The Voice of Romans: The Gospel according to Paul*.[16] Initially, the book was to carry the subtitle "An Adopted Heir"; but after further discussion the decision was made to subtitle the book "The Gospel according to Paul." Various scholars helped the team refine Paul's language in what many claim is the emissary's most important letter.

The Voice New Testament

The first edition of *The Voice New Testament* was subtitled "The Liberating King and His Church."[17] It pulled together the texts and commentaries published previously and combined them with the remaining, unpublished books to complete the New Testament. Each book has a brief introduction and commentary embedded throughout. In all The Voice products, the designers distinguish the commentary from the text of Scripture, but in the full New Testament the ornamentation around the commentary boxes and various colors of ink enhance the look of each page. The Bible was published with two bindings, one paper and the other cloth and soft leather.

blog entry

July 23, 2012

Bible Covers Made in Argentina

by David Capes

Buenos Aires is a study in contrasts. Founded in the 16th century by a small band of Europeans, the city today has 13,000,000 citizens who come from all over the world. It is the wealthiest city in the southern hemisphere, but one-third of its population lives in poverty. Half a million make their home in shanty towns where violence, danger, and deprivation are their daily reality.

In the midst of Argentina's urban darkness La Mision Iglesia Evangelica Presbiteriana offers the light and hope of the gospel. Pastor Marcelo Robles leads a lively community of faith and partners with churches around the world to restore people, their families and communities. Chris Seay and Ecclesia Houston connected with Marcelo several years ago. Together they realized it is better to work together with the poor than simply give them money. The adage is true: "give a man a fish and you feed him for a day; teach him to fish and you feed him for a lifetime." So La Mision has started over twenty micro-enterprises. Each small business provides those willing to work an opportunity to put food on the table, shoes on their feet, and send their children to school with the clothes and supplies they need. The leaders of these businesses teach workers the job skills they need and offer them decent hours and a fair wage. La Mision and its ministry partners are bringing dignity and hope to Buenos Aires.

During one of his visits to Buenos Aires, Chris had an idea. It was 2008 and *The Voice New Testament* had just been published in paperback. La Mision, Chris discovered, has a pastor skilled in leather-working. What if . . . La Mision could start a micro-enterprise that manufactures leather Bible covers for our paperback New Testaments? What if . . . these could be sold in countries of the first world to provide financial help for our brothers and sisters in Argentina? Chris and Marcelo figured out a way to make that happen.

Before long the machines, tools, materials, and people were in place to handcraft some of the most beautiful Bible covers I have ever seen. Workers at La Mision cut and sew the leather. They stamp and carefully stain it in various colors. Each leather Bible cover is one of a kind. Here is a brief video so you can see for yourself the city and the marvelous people making these covers:

http://www.youtube.com/watch?v=_jz7XxcB4L8

In one of the videos, a young man says, "As we make these Bible covers, we pray for those who will one day be reading the Bible." It is beautiful and humbling to think that these brothers and sisters—living at the harsh edge of poverty—would pause from their labors to remember and pray for us who live so well.

Chris' first order was for 500 Bible covers. Chris' second was for 5000. With each Bible cover sold, the buyer receives a beautiful, handcrafted gift and the workers who made it receive a measure of dignity they hadn't known. Wherever the gospel is proclaimed and lived, a part of the world is repaired.

When Thomas Nelson began its plans for publishing the full Bible, they thought of La Mision. What if . . . La Mision could step up their manufacturing and produce leather bindings for the full printed Bible instead of Bible covers for paperbacks? What if . . . those bindings could be shipped to Columbia—where *The Voice Bible* was scheduled to be printed—so the bindings could be glued and sewn on the full Bibles? What if . . . these could be sold in countries of the first world to provide financial help for our brothers and sisters in Argentina? Chris, Marcelo, and the good folks at Thomas Nelson have figured out a way to make that happen.[18]

The Voice Reader's New Testament

Less than a year after the publication of *The Voice New Testament*, Thomas Nelson released *The Voice Reader's New Testament* in paperback.[19] This streamlined version of the translation included the book introductions but not the embedded commentary that made it ideal for public reading in worship. It was also designed for personal devotional reading and evangelism.

The Voice of Psalms

Ecclesia Bible Society commissioned writers and scholars to begin working on the psalms not long after the project began. But since the book of Psalms is so complicated and varied, it took the team a while to resolve all the translation issues so the full text of the Psalter could be published. *The Voice of Psalms*[20] contains the entire book of Psalms in The Voice translation, seventy-five insightful reflections on selected scripture passages, and four reading plans to enhance the reader's time spent in the Psalms. Karen Moore and Frank Couch collaborated on the reflections. Karen, a former employee of Thomas Nelson, is a gifted writer of devotional literature and greeting cards.

The Voice New Testament (revised)

Before the publication of the entire Bible in 2012, the publisher decided to update and revise *The Voice New Testament*.[21] This update came about largely as a result of input provided by scholars and informed readers of the initial publication in 2008. There are over five thousand changes in the revised version, most of which relate to the notes and italicized material. However, there were changes made to the text itself. For example, in the 2008 edition every occurrence of *Christos* in the Greek was translated "Liberating King" or "Liberator" based upon narrative context. This rendering represented a dynamic equivalent of the meaning of the title. But the frequency of the title in the New Testament made the phrase "Liberating King" redundant. So the decision was made to change the translation of *Christos* to "the Anointed," which is more in keeping with the literal meaning of the

123

Greek root. The phrase "Liberating King" was italicized and retained in twenty-six key places in the translation in order to express clearly the reason why God had chosen and anointed Jesus to be His agent. Here are a couple of examples of this change.

The Voice New Testament 2008	The Voice New Testament 2011
Jesus: Ah, but what about you? Who do you say that I am?	Jesus: Ah, but what about you? Who do you say that I am?
Peter: You are the Liberating King sent by God. (Luke 9:20)	Peter: God's Anointed, *the Liberating King*. (Luke 9:20)
With great confidence and with no hindrance, he [Paul] proclaimed the kingdom of God and taught about *the ultimate authority,* Jesus, the promised Liberating King. (Acts 28:31)	With great confidence and with no hindrance, he [Paul] proclaimed the kingdom of God and taught about *the ultimate authority*, Jesus, God's Anointed, *the Liberating King.* (Acts 28:31)
Paul, called out by God's will to be an emissary for Jesus the Liberating King, along with our brother Sosthenes. . . . (1 Corinthians 1:1)	Paul, called out by God's will to be an emissary for Jesus the Anointed, along with our brother Sosthenes. . . . (1 Corinthians 1:1)

Another significant change involved the words *baptize* and *baptism*. Since both words are transliterations and not translations, the initial decision had been to translate all occurrences of the associated Greek roots by phrases such as "ceremonial washing" or "ritual cleansing." This was in keeping with the purposes for which the impure were immersed in water. However, the decision not to include the word *baptism* created confusion in reading certain texts, so in the revised version the word *baptism* is often retained and glossed by additional phrases. Even though the practice of baptism differs widely among Christian communities and the readers initially targeted with this translation may not understand what baptism refers to, the combination of phrases builds an image that most readers can understand. Here are a few examples:

The Voice New Testament 2008	*The Voice New Testament 2011*
That messenger was John the Prophet, who appeared in the desert *near the Jordan River* preaching that people should be ritually cleansed *with water as a sign of* both their changed hearts and God's forgiveness of their sins. (Mark 1:4)	*That messenger was* John the Baptist, who appeared in the desert *near the Jordan River* preaching that people should be ritually cleansed through baptism *with water as a sign of* both their changed hearts and God's forgiveness of their sins. (Mark 1:4)
The jailer brings them to his home, and they have a long conversation with the man and his family. Paul and Silas explain the message of Jesus to them all. The man washes their wounds and *feeds them,* then they ceremonially wash the man and his family. (Acts 16:32)	The jailer brings them to his home, and they have a long conversation with the man and his family. Paul and Silas explain the message of Jesus to them all. The man washes their wounds and *feeds them,* then they baptize the man and his family. (Acts 16:32)
Did someone forget to tell you that when we were initiated into Jesus, the Liberating King, through ceremonial washing, we entered into His death? (Romans 6:3)	Did someone forget to tell you that when we were initiated into Jesus the Anointed through baptism's ceremonial washing, we entered into His death? (Romans 6:3)

The Voice Bible

Though it came a little behind schedule, The Voice Bible was published in the spring 2012. The tag "Step Into the Story of Scripture" continued a theme we had contemplated all along, namely, that the Bible tells a marvelous story of love and redemption and God is inviting us—the readers—to step into that story and make it our own.

As with other Voice-related products, the Bible features (1) contextually equivalent translation; (2) dialogue in screenplay format; (3) supplied words and explanatory paraphrase italicized in the text; (4) introductions to each book; and (5) embedded commentary carefully delineated and located strategically throughout the translation. The front matter of The Voice Bible contains various helps for getting the most out of the translation, an explanation of the translation philosophy, and rationales for some of the translation decisions. In the back matter readers find recommendations for how they can step into the story of Scripture, a spiritual reading strategy known as *lectio divina*, an explanation of the church calendar, several reading plans, topical guides, and colorful maps of the Bible lands.

There was no paperback option for the text of the full Bible. It was published in hardcover, cloth, and several digital formats. The hardcover design for The Voice Bible was created by Scott Lee Designs, a company that had done the covers on all Voice-related projects.

blog entry

August 6, 2012

An Eclectic Translation

by David Capes

A reporter from the Associated Press asked me a question about The Voice translation recently. It was not a question I had heard before, but it was an insightful question. She asked specifically about the translation of Luke 11.

(1) Jesus says to the Pharisees: "You guys don't get it. . . ." (Luke 11:40)

(2) Then, Jesus says to them: "Woe to you, Pharisees. . . ." (Luke 11:42, 43, 44)

She noticed correctly that the first statement has a contemporary ring to it: "You guys don't get it!" But then the translation reverts to a more ancient sound: "Woe to you!" The reporter said, "We don't talk like that today!"

The reporter posed a good question. In those early days [of The Voice project] Chris Seay often used the word "retelling" to describe the method and results. He hoped to retell the biblical stories in ways that are contemporary, ancient, literary, challenging and beautiful.

The mix of contemporary and ancient is part of what sets The Voice apart from other translations. We recognize these texts are ancient, and there is value in building on the wisdom of ages past. There is often a ring, a cadence, a familiarity to ancient language and symbols which still resonates with us. In some places The Voice intentionally retains those words and phrases alongside more contemporary language. Let me give you an example.

Psalm 23 is perhaps the most quoted psalm in the Old Testament. In the King James it reads: "The Lord is my shepherd, I shall not want. . . ." This beloved psalm presents an image and reality we can still grasp. Some may want to contemporize the language and say: "The Lord is my CEO" or "The Lord is my leader." But frankly, that reading sounds strange and leaves us cold. Perhaps a day will come in human history when people no longer retain a memory of our agriculture past and the shepherd's role. Perhaps in that day we will need a more dynamic translation of Psalm 23. Until then, it makes sense to continue to use and celebrate the enduring symbols found in Scripture to say something meaningful about our lives and God's care for us.

In my house we have older furniture as well as modern furniture. Many people today like that eclectic style. I don't think I'd feel comfortable in a house surrounded only by 18th French Provincial or 21st century Modern furniture. It is that mix of wood and glass, of leather and metal, of curved and straight lines, of old and new that fits me, that fits us. It feels like . . . home.[22]

chapter
8

The Story Continues

Every new translation of the Bible must make its way into the already-crowded field of Bible versions. There are more English Bible translations and more copies of the Bible in print than ever before. The Holy Bible in all its translations is the most bought and most owned book in history. But every new translation must find its audience, and The Voice Bible is no exception. With the release of the full Bible in April 2012, the stories of how The Voice is gaining an audience are coming in. We'd like to share a few of those with you.

The Voice in the Media

Not long after The Voice Bible was published, I was driving to the university to teach my classes when I received a phone call from Bob Smietana, a reporter from Nashville's hometown newspaper, the *Tennessean*. Bob was writing an article on the new translation, and he had a number of questions to ask me about the project. I pulled my car into a parking space and walked slowly beneath the live oaks that line the path to my building. As I answered his questions, I got the sense that Bob would write a fair and even account of our project. I'm pleased to say, he did. It was what happened next that was a bit surprising.

His article entitled "Bible Gets New Voice" appeared on Sunday, April 15, 2012, in the *Tennessean*. It began, as many newspaper articles do, with statements designed to attract and hold attention. The same day, an abbreviated version of Bob's article appeared on *USA Today Online* under the title "'The Voice': New Bible translation focuses on dialogue." The same article appeared the next day on page three of the print edition of the paper. It began provocatively:

> The name Jesus Christ doesn't appear in The Voice, a new translation of the Bible. Nor do words such as angel or apostle. Instead, angel is rendered as messenger and apostle as emissary. Jesus Christ is Jesus the Anointed One or the Liberating King.[1]

There are three factual errors in this brief paragraph. First, *Jesus Christ* is not a name; it is a name and a title. *USA Today* proves our point that modern readers mistake *Christ* as a name or part of Jesus' name. There is an important difference between a name and a title. Second, The Voice does not render *angel* as "messenger"; it translates the Greek word *aggelos* as "heavenly messenger." There are, of course, earthly messengers in the Scriptures representing the interests of some earthly authority. We translated these "messengers." Heavenly messengers, however, are distinct in that they come from heaven and represent the interests of heaven on earth. Third, The Voice translates the confession "Jesus Christ"—and it is a confession of faith—consistently as "Jesus the Anointed." The phrase "the Liberating King" is added in italics as an explanatory paraphrase in carefully selected places.

Now if we rely on the newspaper—or any news outlet for that matter—for accuracy, we will soon be disappointed. Often media types don't get the facts right. In truth, they often never even try to get more than a surface understanding of complex subjects such as religion. Setting aside for a moment the factual errors, one is left to ask, what impression was *USA Today* trying to leave with its readership? The answer is obvious.

In the twenty-four-hour news cycle, producers at CNN saw the article and were interested in doing a segment on it. They contacted me Monday afternoon and asked if I would be willing to be interviewed by Carol Costello on CNN the next morning. I agreed and arrived at a local CNN studio in north Houston by 7:30 a.m. on Tuesday.

The interview went well, but it was the way CNN decided to characterize the project during and after the interview that set off a bit of a firestorm. The interview and subsequent articles falsely positioned The Voice as a new Bible translation that leaves out Jesus Christ, angels, and apostles. The title to CNN's online article says it all: "Christ Missing from New Bible."[2] For accuracy sake, it is important to note that the title *Christ* is not in quotation marks in the headline. Had they simply put the word in quotation marks, the statement would be technically correct even if the intent was to give another impression. Still the impression made (intentionally or not) is that The Voice is a new Bible translation that leaves out Jesus, angels, and apostles.

After the CNN interview, I had several other interviews for radio and print media that day and the next. Frank Couch, the executive editor of the project, did some radio interviews as well. Bob Smietana's article showed up in its abbreviated form in about forty media outlets over the next two to three days. I was amazed at how the news spread. As I strolled through the blogosphere, it was interesting to see what a headline like that can do.

A number of scholars who heard about how CNN and *USA Today* misrepresented the project decided to chime in to set the record straight. Larry Hurtado, retired professor of New Testament from the University of Edinburgh, did a post on his blog entitled "On Translation and Hysteria." Larry is a seasoned scholar, sound in judgment, and a warm Christian.

blog entry

April 18, 2012

On Translation and Hysteria

by Larry Hurtado

I've just been alerted to the latest hysterical reaction to translating the NT. (Of course, the week isn't over yet, so we could get something else by Friday!) In the new translation called The Voice Bible (Thomas Nelson Publishers), the choice was made to go for a more dynamic translation of some familiar words. The one that seems to have got some folks all worked up is the translation of the Greek word Christos as "the anointed one". Hysterical people and some news outlets scream: "New translation takes Christ out of the Bible!" So, e.g., the lead scholar in the project, Dr. David Capes (Houston Baptist University), gets interviewed on CNN about why they've done this, and across blog-dom the hysterics spread.

So, for the record: CNN and USA Today have misrepresented the translation. Nobody's removed Jesus from the NT. The translation "anointed" is simply what "Christos" means. It's not a name, of course, but a title.

The translation is from an avowed Evangelical Christian publisher, and Capes is a devout Christian as well as a fine NT scholar. But, because of the hysterical headlines, they're having to spend a lot of time correcting and re-assuring. Some say there's no such thing as bad publicity, but I'm not so sure. Hysterics can be dangerous, like shouting "fire!" in a crowded theatre.

The translation choices of The Voice can be evaluated as to how effective they will be in the intended aim of trying to produce a Bible that can be engaged and understood by the average person who doesn't go to church. But there's no conspiracy to take Jesus out of the Bible or Christian faith. Whew! That's a relief![3]

Darrell Bock, one of the scholars who assisted with the review of Luke-Acts, contributed to an article in the *Christian Post* online: "Theologians OK with Bible Translation Replacing 'Jesus Christ,' 'Angel.'" The article, written by Michael Gryboski, summarizes Bock:

> Bock told The Christian Post that although the word "Christ" does not appear in the text, the meaning of the word is still present in the form of the term "Anointed One," which was frequently used in its place.
>
> "The term was simply not transliterated Christ but explained as anointed one throughout, so there was no change here and Christ is there throughout rendered in the meaning of the term," said Bock. "I do think there can be value in laying out Scripture in a fresh way so people hear it afresh, provided it does not take liberties with the text," said Bock. . . .
>
> "Every effort was made to be careful about how this was done. This is not an effort to conform to American audiences, but is simply rendering the text in a way to makes its meaning clear."[4]

Daniel Kirk, a professor at Fuller Theological Seminary, hosts one of the blogs I like to follow. It is called *Storied Theology*. He is a bright, articulate young scholar. When I told him about the frenzy, he wrote a response entitled: "'Link Bait' and the Voice." *Link bait* is defined at urbandictionary.com as "a headline or title that attracts a high volume of online links. Applies particularly to bloggers hoping to land on the homepage of Digg or Reddit, or anyone hoping that their post will go viral on Twitter."[5] Kirk points out that CNN's use of such an inflammatory title is meant to drive Internet traffic to their site even though it misrepresents what The Voice is all about. As if that were not enough, CNN's online article did something else. Here is how Kirk described it:

> The CNN article also does its CNN thing by linking a totally unrelated commentary piece, written a couple months ago, entitled, "My Take: Stop Sugar Coating the Bible." If you read CNN on a mobile device, these interspersed links are difficult to pick out from the text. There is an implicit commentary created by putting the irrelevant sentence, "My Take: Stop Sugar Coating the Bible" in the middle of a piece about a Bible translation that does not, in fact, sugar coat the Bible as the linked piece complains of.[6]

Martin E. Marty, one of the most important voices in America on religion, heard of the hubbub and invited me to respond on a website he hosts at the University of Chicago. Sponsored by the Martin Marty Center for the Advanced Study of Religion, the twice-weekly posts on *Sightings* seek to report and comment on religion and culture. I entitled my post "The Voice and Media (Mis)Characterization."

blog entry

June 7, 2012

The Voice and Media (Mis)Characterization
by David B. Capes

Martin E. Marty's article "Annenberg Poll on Religion in the Media" brought to our attention a recent survey: "Most Americans Say Media Coverage of Religion Too Sensationalized." I saw that side of the media firsthand. On April 17 I was interviewed by Carol Costello on CNN regarding a new Bible translation I had contributed to called The Voice Bible. The interview and subsequent articles falsely positioned The Voice as a new Bible translation which leaves out Jesus Christ, angels, and apostles. The title to CNN's online article says it all: "Christ Missing from New Bible." Note: no quotation marks.

CNN's interest was prompted by an article the day before in USA Today entitled " 'The Voice': New Bible translation focuses on dialogue." The USA Today article was itself a heavily truncated version of the original story written by Bob Smietana in Nashville's paper, The Tennessean entitled "Bible gets new voice."

Smietana's original article did a fair job of characterizing the project, but as it passed up the media food chain, a significant part of the story was lost, distorted, and sensationalized. By the time CNN covered it, The Voice became a new Bible translation which leaves out Jesus, angels, and the apostles. As one angry fellow said to me: "A Bible without Jesus and the angels! What the heck kind of Bible is that?" Good question.

CNN's (mis)characterization of the translation was based on a half-truth. The word "Christ" is not found in the translation because "Christ" is not a translation at all; it is a transliteration of the Greek word Christos (which means "anointed one"). We translated every occurrence of Christos as "the Anointed" or "the Anointed One." So Jesus is not missing—as CNN's coverage insinuates—He is front and center in this new translation. The translation team did this to clear up a fundamental misunderstanding. Most in the Bible-reading public take the phrase "Jesus Christ" as His name: "Jesus," His first name and "Christ" His last name. In fact, "Christ" is an honorific title like "Son of God," "Lord," and "Savior." But in the western tradition Christos was the only title not translated into the new language of the church. In the Latin Christos was rendered "Christus," and in the English Bible tradition it became "Christ." Our translation decision was intentional: we hoped to recover something of the titular sense of the term in which Jesus the Christos is God's agent, descended from David's royal line, who is chosen ("anointed") and destined to liberate the cosmos from sin, death, oppression, and corruption. We also translated other key terms which happen to be transliterations in all English Bible editions. Words like "apostle" (Greek, apostolos), "baptism" (Greek, baptisma), and "angel" (Greek, angelos) we translated "emissary," "washing," and "heavenly messenger" respectively.

As the blogosphere and airwaves heated up over the media coverage, a number of scholars commented on the sensationalized portrayal of The Voice. Larry Hurtado, retired Professor of New Testament from the University of Edinburgh, wrote an essay on his blog entitled "On Translation and Hysteria," which addressed the media's mischaracterization. On his blog, "Storied Theology," J. Daniel Kirk showed how CNN was baiting the audience with inaccurate information to drive a bit of Internet traffic. Darrell Bock, Kristi Swenson, Edward Fudge, and Greg Garrett also chimed in to set the record straight.

The bottom line is this: both CNN and USA Today misrepresented the project. They either did so intentionally (they wanted to see how Christians might react), out of ignorance (they did not know any better), or out of apathy (they did not care enough to get the story right). Likely it was some combination of the three. As the Annenberg study has shown, those who report on religion are not very knowledgeable of it. And as Martin E. Marty has suggested, those who know enough and care enough to report on religion accurately will most often be met with yawns.[7]

Despite the media's mischaracterizations of The Voice, the overall experience with print, radio, and TV journalists has been positive. As word has gotten out about the project, these reports have provided us many teachable moments to address a wider audience on some central issues about who Jesus is, translation, and culture.

"My new favorite translation"

Since the release of The Voice Bible in April 2012, many people have remarked to me that they now have a new favorite translation. Now, if you have read the earlier chapters carefully, you will realize that we never set out to replace anyone's favorite translation. Our goal has been and continues to be to attract a new audience to the Bible, namely, people who have never read, are reluctant to read, or find the Bible a hard book to understand. We did The Voice for these people. We did it for people like Keith Richards, guitarist for the Rolling Stones, who said, "I read the Bible sometimes, but it bores me to death."[8] In essence, we have been saying all along, "Don't give up, Keith!" We also had in mind a younger demographic, men and women in their twenties and thirties. What we have found, however, is that seasoned Bible readers are hearing God speak to them in fresh, new ways as they take up The Voice and read.

Now some of these enthusiasts seem to have been looking for a new translation. They are quick to pick it up, quick to read it, and quick to love it. Others, however, have taken a little convincing. "A new Bible translation. Bah! Humbug!" That's the gist of what a fellow

The Story Continues

said to Frank Couch and me in the early days of 2012. Frank and I were attending the Justice Conference in Portland, Oregon, talking with people about The Voice Bible. We were also giving away copies of The Voice New Testament to anyone who came by and asked. Most people who stopped by for a brief chat about the project were interested to see what Thomas Nelson and about 120 scholars and writers had been up to for the last seven years. When they discovered the missional purpose of the effort, they walked away with a smile on their faces and a copy or two in their hands. Officials from George Fox University asked for three hundred copies to give to their graduate students. We were only too happy to help. This one fellow, however, was committed to another version. He saw no need—for himself—for a new Bible translation. So his attitude was pretty much, Bah! Humbug!

Well, I'm happy to report, that after a bit of persuasion, the gentleman took a copy of The Voice New Testament back to his hotel room. He came back the next day with a big smile on his face. He said, "I love it. I started reading at 11:00 p.m. and didn't put it down until 1:15 a.m. I read through several books." After spending some time with The Voice, he understood why we had to do this translation. He asked for other copies to give away to friends and family. We were only too happy to help.

What Others Are Saying

The official website of the The Voice Bible, www.hearthevoice.com, contains a number of important resources for those interested in the project. There are videos that describe the project in detail and videos of Scripture portions that artfully portray the written word through visual means. There is a blog that explores various aspects of the translation and our changing culture. There are free downloads, links to various products, and Scripture reading plans. One of the most important items on the official website, however, is the collection of endorsements written by scholars, pastors, and church leaders. Here are a few that give you a sense of what others are saying:

I loved how personal and intimate *The Voice* made the Bible. Stories I'd read a hundred times jumped off the page!

JON ACUFF

WALL STREET JOURNAL BEST-SELLING AUTHOR OF *QUITTER*

AND *STUFF CHRISTIANS LIKE*

There is no book like the Bible and there is no translation like *The Voice*. If you want to walk in the beauty and majesty of Scripture, start here! No other work has been produced by such a unique group of scholars, poets, and musicians. Their work is solid in its scholarship, beautiful in its presentation, and it will stir your heart. An amazing journey awaits. It begins with *The Voice*!

MARK DENISON, D. MIN.

SENIOR PASTOR, FIRST BAPTIST CHURCH, CONROE, TEXAS

God speaks to us through the Bible in a multiplicity of authors, styles, and genres. No single English version can capture all of its power and beauty. *The Voice*, with its translation team of scholars, poets, musicians, and storytellers, captures the rhythm and beauty of Scripture in a unique and creative way. It will greatly enrich your engagement with the Word of God. Highly recommended!

DR. MARK STRAUSS

PROFESSOR OF NEW TESTAMENT, BETHEL SEMINARY, SAN DIEGO

Like most people, I'm sure I have a collection of Bibles that I read from, but *The Voice Bible* has become my new favorite. It is an easy read, and it brings to life through analogies the Word of God. I would have to say my favorite part is handing it off to a fan at a Newsboys concert right after I share a verse from it. . . . The Perfect Gift!

MICHAEL TAIT

NEWSBOYS

The fluid, relevant format of *The Voice* is a great reminder that the Bible isn't a text book or a rule book but a divine love story. As a Bible teacher, I also appreciate the fact this is a translation instead of a paraphrase, which means it's both readable AND theologically reliable. The bottom line is, I think *The Voice* is *the bomb*!

LISA HARPER
WOMEN OF FAITH SPEAKER AND BIBLE TEACHER

The Voice Bible is a choral masterpiece. Finally a choir of original voices contribute to a translation designed to meet the most exacting scholarly standards while resonating with as wide a readership as possible.

LEONARD SWEET
DREW UNIVERSITY, GEORGE FOX UNIVERSITY,
CHIEF CONTRIBUTOR TO SERMONS.COM

I *LOVE* it!!!!!! I've always been pretty traditional when it comes to my Bible translations. I've basically read the same translation for the past 36 years of my life. *The Voice* is the first translation that has made me audibly say "Wow." It's fresh, enlightening, and extremely accurate.

PETE WILSON
AUTHOR AND PASTOR AT CROSSPOINT CHURCH, NASHVILLE, TENNESSEE

I really love *The Voice*. I can hardly put it down! I've read over 25 translations of the New Testament (incuding KJ, NKJ, AMP, RSV, NIV, ASV, Living Bible, Aramaic, Koine Greek, Kenneth Wuest, and more). I can't wait to finish this new version (I am now in Acts) so I can do a full review. I have always been a fan of the King James Version, but I believe this REVOLUTIONARY Bible is for today. I can certainly tell that much prayer and dedication was made to make this precious Word alive for this generation. There is equanimity on every page. The narrative is great in the gospels. The italics are very cleverly inserted and is more convenient than having a bulky (sometimes

Calvinist-influenced) commentary. When I read John 1:1 (and the prelude) I found out the reason for the title and I was blown away! I like many Bibles for study, but if I only had one, this would be it! Thank God for your team, I have been waiting for a Bible like this for a long time! I am now using *The Voice* for my ministry website's "weekly verse."

REV. JEFF LOWE
COTTONWOOD CHURCH, CYPRESS, CALIFORNIA

Translating for *The Voice* put me in touch with the Bible in new ways, both intimate and playful. Working so closely with the Hebrew texts reminded me again of their multivalency and the importance of a project like this. It gives readers a firsthand sense of the many voices that populate God's Word, and it allows possibilities for conveying meaning not bound by one-to-one translation. Given room by VOICE editors to reach within our own language, I could strive for a living text—evocative, poignant, inspirational, disturbing, and comforting—some of the many ways that the biblical texts mean most powerfully.

KRISTIN M. SWENSON, PHD
RESEARCH PROFESSOR IN RELIGIOUS STUDIES
UNIVERSITY OF VIRGINIA

If it is true that the Word of God is alive and active, and if it is also true that many people have not experienced the Bible as a life-giving text, then *The Voice* can help bridge that gap. Contemporary language, format, and insight make *The Voice* a wonderful place to hear the old, old story in fresh ways—and in that story to encounter the living God.

MICHAEL J. GORMAN, PHD
THE ECUMENICAL INSTITUTE OF THEOLOGY
ST. MARY'S SEMINARY & UNIVERSITY

Rather than imposing a flat, artificial style on the entire Bible, *The Voice* allows the unique personalities of the biblical writers to shine through their texts. Various features are included to help us "feel" as well as hear scriptural speech and dialogue. Readers experience the Bible as the living word.

KENNETH L. WATERS SR., PHD
ASSOCIATE DEAN OF THE DIVISION OF RELIGION
AND PHILOSOPHY AND PROFESSOR OF NEW TESTAMENT
AZUSA PACIFIC UNIVERSITY

The Bible informs the intellect about God, the world, and ourselves, but it is more than an information book. God is interested in us as whole people, so His Word also stimulates our imagination, arouses our emotions, and appeals to our will. *The Voice* combines the skills of biblical scholars with the sensitivities of musicians, novelists, and poets, and the result is an accurate and stimulating English translation that readers will find hard to put down. Long-time as well as new readers will benefit greatly from their experience of *The Voice*.

TREMPER LONGMAN, PHD
ROBERT H. GUNDRY PROFESSOR OF BIBLICAL STUDIES
WESTMONT COLLEGE

As one who worked on the *The Voice*—and did so entering in with some skepticism—I can say that much care was given to be accurate as pastors and scholars were teamed up to produce the text. That care is still being shown. As an explanatory paraphrase, a genre with a rich history in biblical translation, *The Voice* can open up the point of the text in effective ways. This also means it is being checked and reevaluated to make it even better in bringing out the force of the text. With such a commitment to reflecting the text, this translation can serve the church well and help people appreciate the richness of the message of Scripture.

DARRELL BOCK, PHD
RESEARCH PROFESSOR OF NEW TESTAMENT STUDIES
DALLAS THEOLOGICAL SEMINARY

I have been involved in *The Voice* project for over five years. Many might well ask, "Why do we need yet another Bible translation?" Why? The Bible is an amazingly transparent and yet amazingly puzzling document. Theologians have been translating and interpreting it for millennia, and I daresay they will continue to do so for millennia to come. *The Voice* represents a new "voice" in the translation and interpretation undertaking, one that genuinely attempts to make the text accessible to the reader of the twenty-first century. Read it for yourself; better, engage it for yourself. Let it draw you in; let it speak to you. And discover in its words "the voice" of the biblical text.

NANCY L. deCLAISSÉ-WALFORD, PhD
PROFESSOR OF OLD TESTAMENT AND BIBLICAL LANGUAGES
McAFEE SCHOOL OF THEOLOGY, MERCER UNIVERSITY

Step into the Story

A lot of stories end, "and they lived happily ever after." But the story of the Bible never ends. Now don't misunderstand, the canon is closed; no books will be added, none taken away. Still God's invitation is open. God continually calls us to step into the story of Scripture and make it our own. God is inviting us to enter into a new covenant inaugurated by Jesus, to see Abraham as our father, David and his father Jesse as our kin, and people of faith across the ages as our brothers and sisters. The story of love and redemption—the story of how God is repairing the world—begins not long after Adam and Eve disobey God in the garden and will continue until the day when "all things" are reconciled to God (Colossians 1:15). That renewal has begun. The church is to be a community of reconciled people working to reconcile the rest of the world to God through Jesus the Anointed. We read about the heroes of faith in the Scripture. We see in them our hopes and our faults. What they started, we are to continue. It is our turn. The torch has been passed. It is our job to run the race of faith well and hand it on to the next generation.

So the story continues . . .

In the second century AD, Justin Martyr, one of the early church leaders, described what Jesus' followers did when they gathered for worship. On the day of the Sun, he said, all who lived in the cities and country would gather together in one place. They read aloud the Gospels—literally, "the memoirs of the apostles"—and the prophets "as long as time permits." Then when the reader was finished, the president of the congregation would rise to instruct the disciples and encourage them to imitate the noble things they heard in Scripture.[9]

I come from a tradition where the average Sunday morning sermon consists of one minute of Scripture—often poorly read—followed by thirty minutes of pastoral commentary—often having little or nothing to do with the Scripture just read. I'd love to see a change in how churches engage Scripture. Why not turn it around and have thirty minutes of Scripture followed by a minute or two of the pastor's encouragement to hear God's Voice and let the Spirit speak and the church act on it? I say that not only as one who speaks but as one who listens. In worship I'd much prefer to hear the Scriptures read well, the stories dramatized, and the Psalms put to music than to hear many of the sermons I've preached or listened to through the years.

The Voice Bible is a tool that can help us make that happen.

notes

Chapter 1: In the Beginning

1. David B. Capes, "The Power of the Story Reaches Us," *Hear the Voice* (blog), September 26, 2011, http://www.hearthevoice.com/blog/2.

2. David Capes, "The Voice and The Message," *Hear the Voice* (blog), May 4, 2012, http://www.hearthevoice.com/blog/25.

3. Chris Seay, *The Tao of Enron: Spiritual Lessons from a Fortune 500 Fallout* (Colorado Springs: NavPress, 2002).

4. Greg Garrett, *Free Bird* (New York: Kensington, 2003); Greg Garrett, *Cycling: A Novel* (New York: Kensington, 2003).

5. Chris Seay and Greg Garrett, *The Gospel Reloaded: Exploring Spirituality and Faith in* The Matrix (Colorado Springs: Pinon, 2003).

6. Donald Miller, *Blue Like Jazz: Nonreligious Thoughts on Christian Spirituality* (Nashville: Thomas Nelson, 2003); Donald Miller, *Searching for God Knows What* (Nashville: Thomas Nelson, 2004).

Chapter 2: The Development Team

1. John Eames, in conversation with the author, January 2012.

2. David Capes, "The Most Interesting Man in the World," *Hear the Voice* (blog), April 9, 2012, http://www.hearthevoice.com/blog/15.

3. Misty Bourne, "Remembering Merrie," *Hear the Voice* (blog), November 21, 2011, http://hearthevoice.com/blog/6.

4. David Capes, "Kelly 'Black Arrow,'" *Hear the Voice* (blog), May 18, 2012, http://www.hearthevoice.com/blog/28.

Chapter 3: The Version Title

1. Greg Garrett, in conversation with the author, July 2012.

2. Gordon D. Fee and Mark L. Strauss, *How to Choose a Translation*

for All Its Worth: A Guide to Understanding and Using Bible Versions (Grand Rapids: Zondervan, 2007), 47–48.
3. David Capes, "The Bible in 4-D!" Hear the Voice (blog), January 3, 2012, http://www.hearthevoice.com/blog/10.

Chapter 4: The Translation Philosophy

1. Alister McGrath, In the Beginning: The Story of the King James Bible and How It Changed a Nation, a Language, and a Culture (New York: Anchor, 2002), 254–55.
2. Greek-English Lexicon of the New Testament Based on Semantic Domains, ed. Johannes P. Louw and Eugene A. Nida (New York: United Bible Societies, 1988), s.v. "apostolos."

Chapter 5: Contextual Equivalence in Practice

1. Carl Sagan, Pale Blue Dot: A Vision of the Human Future in Space (New York: Ballantine, 1994).
2. W. Sibley Town, "The Book of Ecclesiastes," in The New Interpreter's Bible, ed. Leander Keck, vol. 5 (Nashville: Abingdon, 1997).
3. We are referring here specifically to the phrase dikaiosunē theou in Paul's letters. The language of "righteousness" means other things in other places. For example, in the Sermon on the Mount "righteousness" has more of an ethical, moral bent. In Matthew 6 it has to do with the right (versus wrong) way to pray, fast, and give to the poor. It is clearly an interior matter for Jesus, however, and not just about external performance.
4. John Newton, "Faith's Review and Expectation" ["Amazing Grace"], 1779.
5. Jack Wisdom, "The Bogus World System," Hear the Voice (blog), July 12, 2012, http://www.hearthevoice.com/blog/37.

Chapter 6: The Divine Name

1. The Jerusalem Bible, by Alexander Jones (London: Darton, Longman and Todd and Doubleday, 1966).

2. American Standard Bible (1901); Young's Literal Translation, by Robert Young (Grand Rapids: Baker, 1898).

3. James Moffatt, *A New Translation of The Bible Containing the Old and New Testaments*, rev. ed. (1935; New York: Harper and Row, 1954), xxi.

4. *Complete Jewish Bible: An English Version by David H. Stern* (Clarksville, MD: Messianic Jewish Publisher, 1998).

Chapter 7: The Product Line

1. Chris Seay and David Capes, *The Last Eyewitness: The Final Week* (Nashville: Thomas Nelson, 2006).

2. Seay and Capes, back cover to *Last Eyewitness*.

3. David Capes, "A Londoner at the Astros Game," *Hear the Voice* (blog), June 16, 2012, http://www.hearthevoice.com/blog/32.

4. *Songs from The Voice*, vol. 1, Derek Webb, Robbie Seay Band, et al., Thomas Nelson, 2006, cd.

5. *Songs from The Voice*, vol. 2, Thomas Nelson, 2006, cd.

6. Brian McLaren, *The Dust Off Their Feet: Lessons from the First Church* (Nashville: Thomas Nelson, 2006).

7. Brian McLaren, *The Voice of Luke: Not Even Sandals* (Nashville: Thomas Nelson, 2007).

8. Lauren Winner, *The Voice of Matthew* (Nashville: Thomas Nelson, 2007).

9. David Capes, "A Remarkable Day," *Hear the Voice* (blog), November 28, 2012, http://www.hearthevoice.com/blog/61.

10. Chris Seay, Brian McLaren, et al., *The Voice from On High: God Announces His Son as Israel's Liberating King* (Nashville: Thomas Nelson, 2007), 3.

11. Chris Seay, *The Voice Revealed: The True Story of the Last Eyewitness* (Nashville: Thomas Nelson, 2007).

12. Greg Garrett and David Capes, *The Voice of Hebrews: The Mystery of Melchizedek* (Nashville: Thomas Nelson, 2008).

13. Scott Lee, "A Memorable Cover: *The Voice of Hebrews*," *Hear the Voice* (blog), August16, 2012, http://www.hearthevoice.com/blog/42.

14. David Capes, "A Few Days in Austin," *Hear the Voice* (blog), August 27, 2012, http://www.hearthevoice.com/blog/44.

15. Greg Garrett and Matthew Paul Turner, *The Voice of Mark: Let Them Listen* (Nashville: Thomas Nelson, 2008).

16. Chris Seay, David B. Capes, Kelly Hall, *The Voice of Romans: The Gospel According to Paul* (Nashville: Thomas Nelson, 2008).

17. *The Voice New Testament* (Nashville: Thomas Nelson, 2008).

18. David Capes, "Bible Covers Made in Argentina," *Hear the Voice* (blog), July 23, 2012, http://www.hearthevoice.com/blog/39.

19. *The Voice Reader's New Testament* (Nashville: Thomas Nelson, 2009).

20. Ecclesia Bible Society, *The Voice of Psalms* (Nashville: Thomas Nelson, 2009).

21. *The Voice New Testament*, rev. ed. (Nashville: Thomas Nelson, 2011).

22. David Capes, "An Eclectic Translation," *Hear the Voice* (blog), August 6, 2012, http://www.hearthevoice.com/blog/40.

Chapter 8: The Story Continues

1. Bob Smietana, "'The Voice': New Bible translation focuses on Dialogue, *USA Today*, April 16, 2012, http://usatoday30.usatoday.com/news/religion/story/2012-04-15/the-voice-bible-translation/54301502/1.

2. "Christ Missing from New Bible," CNN Newsroom, April 17, 2012, http://www.cnn.com/video/#/video/bestoftv/2012/04/17/sot-nr-the-voice-bible.cnn.

3. Larry Hurtado, "On Translation and Hysteria," *Larry Hurtado's Blog*, April 18, 2012, http://larryhurtado.wordpress.com/2012/04/18/on-translation-and-hysteria/.

4. Michael Gryboski, "Theologicans OK with Bible Translation Replacing 'Jesus Christ,' 'Angel,'" *Christian Post*, Church and Ministries, April 19, 2012, http://www.christianpost.com/news/theologians-ok-with-bible-translation-replacing-jesus-christ-angel-73556/.

5. *Urban Dictionary*, s.v. linkbait, http://www.urbandictionary.com/define.php?term=linkbait.

6. Daniel Kirk, "'Link Bait' and the Voice," *Storied Theology* (blog),

April 18, 2010, http://www.jrdkirk.com/2012/04/18/ link-bait-and-the-voice/.

7. David B. Capes, "The Voice and Media (Mis)Characterization," *Sightings* (blog), June 7, 2012, http://divinity.uchicago.edu/ martycenter/publications/sightings/archive_2012/0607.shtml.

8. Alex Fletcher, "Keith Richards: 'The Bible is boring,'" *Digital Spy*, March 10, 2008; http://www.digitalspy.com/celebrity/news/a91198/ keith-richards-the-bible-is-boring.html.

9. "67: Weekly Worship of the Chistians," *St. Justin Martyr: The First and Second Apologies*, ed. Leslie W. Barnard (New York: Paulist, 1997), 71.

about the authors

David B. Capes is the Thomas Nelson Research Professor at Houston Baptist University. He is the senior Bible scholar reviewing The Voice, a Scripture project to rediscover the story of the Bible. He is the author and editor of a number of books, including *The Last Eyewitness: The Final Week*, *The Voice of Hebrews: The Mystery of Melchizedek*, *Rediscovering Paul*, and *Thriving in Babylon*.

Chris Seay is a church planter, pastor, president of Ecclesia Bible Society, and internationally acclaimed speaker. His six previous books include *The Gospel According to Lost*, *The Gospel According to Tony Soprano*, and *Faith of My Fathers*.

James F. Couch Jr. is the associate publisher for Thomas Nelson Publishers for Reference, Curriculum, and Translation Development. He has edited nine study Bibles in his career and shares the pulpit in his church with two other teaching ministers.